Living Values Activities
for Children
Ages 3–7

# Living Values Activities for Children Ages 3–7

DEVELOPED AND WRITTEN BY
**Diane Tillman and Diana Hsu**

WITH ADDITIONAL ACTIVITIES FROM
Dominique Ache
Encarnación Royo Costa
Marcia Maria Lins de Medeiros
Max and Marcia Nass
and other educators around the world

**Health Communications, Inc.**
**Deerfield Beach, Florida**

*www.hci-online.com*

Visit the Living Values Web site for trainings at *http://www.livingvalues.net.*

**Library of Congress Cataloging-in-Publication Data**

Tillman, Diane

    Living Values activities for children ages 3–7 / developed and written by Diane Tillman and
Diana Hsu; with additional activities from Dominique Ache . . . [et al.].

    p.   cm.

    ISBN 1-55874-879-2 (trade paper : alk. paper)

    1. Moral education (Early childhood) 2. Living Values, an Educational Program. 3. Values—Study
and teaching (Early childhood)—Activity programs. I. Hsu, Diana. II. Title.

LB1139.35.M67 T55 2000
372'.01'14—dc21

                                      00-061335

Living Values: An Educational Program is a partnership among educators around the world. This program is supported by UNESCO and sponsored by the Spanish Committee of UNICEF, the Planet
Society, and the Brahma Kumaris, in consultation with the Educational Cluster of UNICEF (New York).

Publisher: Health Communications, Inc.
              3201 S.W. 15th Street
              Deerfield Beach, FL 33442-8190

*Cover and inside book design by Lawna Patterson Oldfield*
*Inside and cover artwork by Frow Steeman*
*Original editor Carol Gill*

# CONTENTS

## SETTING THE CONTEXT

The Call for Values ...........................................................................vii

What Kind of Program Is LVEP? ..........................................................vii

## INTRODUCTION

Teaching Values ................................................................................xi

Where Do I Begin? ...........................................................................xiii

Recommended Order of Values Units...................................................xiii

A Variety of Values Activities .............................................................xiv

Bringing in the Values of Your Culture................................................xvii

Using the Values Units .....................................................................xviii

Acknowledging Responses ..................................................................xx

Symbols Used Throughout the Lessons.................................................xxi

Educators—Share with the World!........................................................xxii

## VALUES UNITS

1. Peace ............................................................................................1

2. Respect .........................................................................................31

3. Love .............................................................................................59

4. Responsibility ............................................................ 83

5. Happiness ................................................................. 99

6. Cooperation .............................................................. 121

7. Honesty ................................................................... 139

8. Humility .................................................................. 151

9. Tolerance ................................................................. 165

10. Simplicity ............................................................... 177

11. Unity .................................................................... 187

## APPENDIX

| | | |
|---|---|---|
| Item 1: Peace | The Star Story | 197 |
| Item 2: Respect | Lily the Leopard | 201 |
| Item 3: Love | The Happy Sponges | 204 |
| Item 4: Responsibility | The Seed | 206 |
| Item 5: Happiness | The Heart School | 209 |
| Item 6: Honesty | The Emperor and the Flower Seeds | 219 |
| Item 7: Happiness | Billy the Bully | 223 |
| Item 8: Tolerance | Josh the Dragon | 226 |
| Quietly Being Exercises | All Values | 229 |

Cited Books and Songs ................................................... 231

Acknowledgments ......................................................... 233

About the Authors ......................................................... 235

# SETTING THE CONTEXT

## The Call for Values

Children around the world are increasingly affected by violence, growing social problems and a lack of respect for each other and the world around them. Parents and educators in many countries are asking for help to turn around this alarming trend. Many of them believe part of the solution is an emphasis on teaching values. Living Values: An Educational Program (LVEP) has been produced in response to this call for values.

## What Kind of Program Is LVEP?

Living Values: An Educational Program (LVEP) is a values education program. It offers a variety of experiential activities and practical methodologies for teachers and facilitators to help children and young adults explore and develop twelve key personal and social values: Peace, Respect, Love, Responsibility, Happiness, Cooperation, Honesty, Humility, Tolerance, Simplicity and Unity. LVEP also contains special segments for use with parents and caregivers, as well as for refugees and children affected by war. As of March 2000, LVEP was already in use at over 1800 sites in 64 countries. Reports from educators indicate that students are responsive to the values activities and become interested in discussing and applying values. Teachers note that students appear more confident, are more respectful to others and exhibit an increase in positive and cooperative personal and social skills.

## The Aims of LVEP:

- To help individuals think about and reflect on different values and the practical implications of expressing them in relation to themselves, others, the community and the world at large.
- To deepen understanding, motivation and responsibility with regard to making positive personal and social choices.
- To inspire individuals to choose their own personal, social, moral and spiritual values and be aware of practical methods for developing and deepening them.
- To encourage educators and caregivers to look at education as providing students with a philosophy of living, thereby facilitating their overall growth, development and choices so they may integrate themselves into the community with respect, confidence and purpose.

## Current Status

LVEP is a nonprofit entity which is a partnership among educators around the world. It is currently supported by UNESCO and sponsored by the Spanish Committee of UNICEF, the Planet Society and the Brahma Kumaris, in consultation with the Education Cluster of UNICEF (New York).

This book contains values activities for children ages three to seven. Other components of Living Values: An Educational Program include five additional books: *Living Values Activities for Children Ages 8–14; Living Values Activities for Young Adults; LVEP Educator Training Guide; Living Values Parent Groups;*

*A Facilitator Guide*, and *Living Values Activities for Refugees and Children Affected by War.*

Educators around the world are encouraged to utilize their own rich heritage while integrating values into everyday activities and the curriculum.

In the LVEP series, reflective and visualization activities encourage students to access their own creativity and inner gifts. Communication activities teach students to implement peaceful social skills. Artistic activities, songs and movement inspire students to express themselves while experiencing the value of focus. Game-like activities are thought-provoking and fun; the discussion time that follows those activities helps students explore effects of different attitudes and behaviors. Other activities stimulate awareness of personal and social responsibility and social justice. The development of self-esteem and tolerance continues throughout the exercises.

LVEP materials have been translated into many languages. The current set of six books was developed from the *Living Values Educators' Kit,* originally available in English, French and Spanish. The expanded edition of the six LVEP books is currently available in English. Translation is ongoing in Arabic, Chinese, German, Greek, Hebrew, Hungarian, Italian, Japanese, Karen, Malay, Polish, Portuguese, Russian, Spanish, Thai, Turkish and Vietnamese.

## Background

LVEP grew out of an international project begun in 1995 by the Brahma Kumaris to celebrate the fiftieth anniversary of the United Nations. Called *Sharing Our Values for a Better World,* this project focused on twelve universal values. The theme—adopted from a tenet in the Preamble of the United Nations' Charter—was: *"To reaffirm faith in fundamental human rights, in the dignity and worth of the human person. . . ."*

*Living Values: A Guidebook* was created as part of this project. It provided value statements on the twelve core values, offered an individual perspective for creating and sustaining positive change, and included facilitated group workshops and activities, including a small section of values activities for students in the classroom. That sketchy classroom curriculum became the inspiration and impetus for Living Values: An Education Initiative (LVEI).

LVEI was born when twenty educators from around the world gathered at UNICEF Headquarters in New York City in August of 1996 to discuss the needs of children, their experiences of working with values, and how educators can integrate values to better prepare students for lifelong learning. Using *Living Values: A Guidebook* and the "Convention on the Rights of the Child" as a framework, the global educators identified and agreed upon the purpose and aims of values-based education worldwide, in both developed and developing countries. The *Living Values Educators' Kit* was ready for piloting in February of 1997, and Living Values has been gaining momentum ever since.

# INTRODUCTION

## Teaching Values

These values-based activities for children aged three through seven incorporate a variety of ways to explore values. Learning new concepts, sharing and thinking, creating, and teaching social skills are combined with playing, art, singing, movement and imagining. The values activities can be used by elementary school teachers, nursery and preschool teachers, parents, caregivers and daycare center staff. Adults involved are integral to the success of the program, for children learn best by example and are most receptive when what is shared is experienced. Patience, love and seeing the beauty of every child are important and invaluable aspects. These will be your gifts to the children as you do these activities. Your behavior will enable the children to experience these values as their own and to use them in their interactions with others.

Our experience has been that children of this age are especially receptive to cooperative ways of interacting and a values-based atmosphere. They enjoy learning about the values and learn positive social communication skills easily. Children function at their best in a nurturing environment of respect, patience and clear rules rather than of blame, shame and anger. They enjoy expressing their thoughts and feelings and being acknowledged. Their vocabulary, ability to think constructively and critical thinking skills develop along with social skills, emotional growth and self-esteem.

## Three Core Assumptions

There are three core assumptions upon which LVEP is built:

1. Universal values teach respect and dignity for each and every person. Learning to enjoy those values promotes well-being for individuals and the larger society.
2. Each student does care about values and has the capacity to positively create and learn when provided with opportunities.
3. Students thrive in a values-based atmosphere in a positive, safe environment of mutual respect and care; where students are regarded as capable of learning to make socially conscious choices.

## LVEP Trainings

The creation of a values-based atmosphere facilitates the success of this program, making it more enjoyable, beneficial and effective for both students and teachers. During LVEP trainings, educators participate in values awareness sessions. They are asked to reflect on their own values, offer their ideas on elements within a values-based atmosphere and imagine an optimal classroom environment. After teachers discuss their ideas on best teaching practices, LVEP's theoretical model and the rationale behind the variety of values activities are presented. This is followed by one or more sessions engaged in LVEP values activities for children and/or young adults. The workshop then turns to skills for creating a values-based environment: acknowledgement, encouragement and positively building behaviors; active listening; conflict resolution; collaborative rule making; and values-based discipline.

# Where Do I Begin?

There are activities on eleven values in this book. They are Peace, Respect, Love, Responsibility, Happiness, Cooperation, Honesty, Humility, Tolerance, Simplicity and Unity.

The LVEP values activities for children this age are short; twenty minutes is usually sufficient. The activities can be easily incorporated into opening time, circle time or language arts. Values are naturally reinforced during the entire day when the school chooses to focus on a value for a particular period of time and the educators are committed to a values-based atmosphere.

It is recommended that all educators begin with the Peace and Respect units. There are twenty-two lessons in each of these two units. The Quietly Being exercises and conflict resolution skills developed during these first forty-four lessons are important building blocks in creating both a values-based atmosphere and positive social skills. Do the lessons in order.

# Recommended Order of Values Units

Peace

Respect

Love

Responsibility

Happiness

Cooperation

Honesty

Humility

Tolerance

Simplicity

Unity

The teacher may note that the LVEP books for older children and young adults contain lessons for a twelfth value, Freedom. It is felt that a values-based atmosphere itself will create the feeling of freedom for children of this age. Freedom is introduced more formally with Living Values Activities at the eight- to fourteen-year-old level. However, the *Living Values Parent Groups: A Facilitator Guide* briefly addresses the value of Freedom and its application for three- through seven-year-olds.

## Can We Do the Values in a Different Order?

It is important for each teacher, school, and/or school system to look at the needs of children and develop a program tailored to the particular setting. Always, however, start with the Peace unit and follow that with the Respect unit, as these first lessons contain essential skills used throughout the other lessons.

# A Variety of Values Activities

It is not enough for children to hear about values. To really learn, they must experience them at many different levels, making them their own. And it is not enough to feel, experience and think about the values; social skills are needed to be able to use values throughout the day. The youngsters of today increasingly need to be able to see the effects of their behaviors and choices and be able to develop socially conscious decision-making skills.

## Reflection Points

The Reflection Points define values in simple ways for young children. Different points are discussed during the lessons. The teacher may wish to add a few of his or her own Reflection Points or use favorite sayings from the culture of the community.

In addition to defining values, the Reflection Points offer a values perspective, that is, one of valuing the dignity and worth of each human being. For example, one Reflection Point in the unit on Respect for ages three through seven is: Respect is knowing I am unique and valuable. Another is: Respect is knowing others are valuable, too.

## Imagining

A few values units ask children to imagine a peaceful world or a happy world. For example, students visualizing a peaceful world are asked to share their experiences and then draw or paint a picture. This imagination exercise not only elicits the creativity of "good students," but also interests students often considered resistant or "unmotivated." Visualizations make the values more relevant to students as they find a place from within where they experience that quality and create ideas they know are their own. Many of the values exercises require positive acknowledgement of children's responses.

## Quietly Being Exercises

Very often children do not like "having to be quiet" in school. They seem to experience it as having to curtail their fun and repress their energy and enjoyment. It is viewed not as something enjoyable, but as something necessary to do in order to comply with adult requests.

The first values unit on Peace has a story about Peace Stars. The children are introduced to the practice of enjoying being silent and peaceful like the stars. The Respect and the Love units also have Quietly Being exercises. These are designed to help the children enjoy "feeling" the value. Teachers have found that doing these exercises helps children quiet down, be more content and concentrate more successfully on their studies. After Lesson 44, it is suggested that the teacher do a Quietly Being exercise daily. As you continue, allow the children to make up their own Quietly Being exercises.

## Artistic Expression

Children are encouraged to reflect about values and experience them artistically and creatively through the arts. They paint peace, create songs and dance cooperation. Little children make wings representing humility and self-respect, then sing a related song as they move in a circle. While some songs are included, teachers are encouraged to bring in the traditional songs of their culture or the cultures represented in the area and to sing those with the children.

## Self-Development Activities

In these activities, students explore the value in relation to themselves or build skills in relation to the value. For example, in the Peace unit, children use puppets to enact their peaceful world. In the Respect unit, students look at their own as well as others' positive qualities. During an activity in the Honesty unit, children examine their feelings when they are honest. There are a few stories about values, and teachers are invited to bring in their favorite stories on the unit of focus.

## Social Skills

The Peace unit has several lessons on conflict resolution. The Respect and Love units continue developing these skills. In the unit on Love, children explore concepts such as "giving flowers rather than thorns." The Cooperation unit's games are fun, yet also elicit social communication skills.

## Developing Skills for Social Cohesion

The units on Tolerance, Simplicity and Unity bring in elements of social responsibility which are interesting and fun. Using colors of the rainbow as an analogy, children explore the variety of cultures. The unit on Simplicity includes suggestions for conservation and respect for the earth. Students explore positive examples of unity and then work together on a project of their choice.

## Incorporating Values into the Existing Curriculum

Introductory sessions, circle time, language arts and social studies lead easily to an exploration of values, as do the arts. Teams of teachers can brainstorm values applications at their particular site or in their subject areas. The values lessons are brief, however, and many teachers enjoy doing them at the beginning of the day.

# Bringing in the Values of Your Culture

It is our hope that these activities will elicit ideas from teachers and parents as they explore with children the variety of ways to experience and develop values. This material is intended to be a stimulus. Adapt it to your group of students. Use your own resources and creativity. Bring in stories, songs and games from your culture and the cultures within and around your country to illustrate values. Use materials that are easily available. Use your creativity, skills and knowledge to continue values-based education.

The songs included are available on cassette. However, since some of your children may not speak English, you may wish to translate the words or use songs from your own culture or different cultures from around the world. Ask the children to create their own plays and songs. They might even want to do a skit. Perhaps older adults can tell traditional tales and teach ancient forms of music. Send us your favorite values stories and activities!

# Using the Values Units

## Peace and Respect Units—the First 44 Lessons

Begin with Lesson 1 in the Peace unit. Values activities on peace continue through Lesson 22. There are another 22 lessons on the value of Respect. In each lesson, there is a discussion time and an activity. Reflection Points, songs and Quietly Being exercises are gradually introduced. By the end of Lesson 44, the children will know a few songs and be familiar with two Quietly Being exercises (the Peace Star exercise and the Respect Star exercise), as well as a variety of values activities.

## After the Peace and Respect Lessons

1. **Sing.** Begin or end with a song, as you prefer. Sing songs on the theme of the value with the children, but include the Peace, Respect and Love songs occasionally.

2. **Quietly Being Exercises.** Do a Quietly Being exercise once a day. Initially the teacher may wish to alternate daily between the Peace Star exercise and the Respect Star exercise. After the class has completed the

Love unit, do the Filling Up with Love exercise every third lesson. For your convenience, these exercises are also in the Appendix. As the values lessons proceed, other exercises are introduced, and you may wish to allow the children to make up some of their own.

3. **Lesson.** Do one lesson daily, or whatever your schedule permits. Lessons often include a discussion as well as an activity. They are in the recommended order. Feel free to be creative and add your own ideas as well as activities from the culture(s) of the children. For this age group the values lessons can be very short; twenty minutes is sufficient.

4. **Circle Time.** Try to provide circle or sharing time once a day, or, if not possible, once a week. Circle time is an excellent beginning for values time. The children can sit in a circle if there are fewer than fifteen, or if more, they can be grouped in front of the teacher. Ask what they feel good about today or what they are proud of. Or ask them to tell how they showed love or peace to someone. Positively acknowledge whatever they share. It is a good time to engage in collaborative rule changes and conflict resolution as needed.

## Adapt the Level of Language to Different Ages

Educators will need to adapt the level of language, directions and the amount of adult assistance to the age of the children. That is especially important for this age range, as language and directions for a three-year-old are simpler and more concrete than for a seven-year-old. Some of the activities can also be adapted for two-year-olds. One of the authors initially did some of the activities she developed with two-year-olds, and they responded very positively.

## Values Assemblies

If the entire school is exploring the same value for a period of time, a short assembly is often an excellent way to start. A few teachers could create the first program. After that, different classes of children could take turns doing a song and a skit. Or, the principal may wish to tell a story and involve a few children from the audience.

# Acknowledging Responses

Occasionally there are students who are resistant to school and/or school-work, and that may include values activities initially. Part of resistance may be anger at not being heard and at not feeling adequate or valued. Part of the success of these values activities is acceptance of each student.

Acceptance and acknowledgment of students' responses are essential components of many discussions that take place as part of the values activities. This may pose a challenge to teachers who are accustomed to having only "right" or "wrong" answers in the classroom. While there are "right" and "wrong" answers in math and science, for instance, a student's emotional feeling about a concept is simply his or her own.

Resistant students may initially test the acceptance of their answers by giving nonstandard responses. For example, when asked about a peaceful world, a student might say, "War has to be part of a peaceful world." Or, in response to a question in the Happiness unit about what he or she likes to hear, a student might respond, "I like to hear that I am bad." Simply consider these responses as reflections of the student's unhappiness. Nod with respect, just as you did to the other students.

It is sufficient to nod, but a verbal response acknowledging the student's answer and restating the content of his or her message is a more effective method of giving respect. Consistently receiving respect from an adult in this way frees the student from the trap of blaming the adult for not understanding. Actively listening to such responses allows the student to accept his or her emotions and begin to process them. For example, if the child draws guns in her picture of a peaceful world, the teacher might say in an accepting manner, if the child's face seems tense, "It must be a little scary if there are guns even in a peaceful world." (Please refer to the section on Active Listening in the *LVEP Educator Training Guide* for more on this topic.)

It is important for the educator to be consistent in modeling his or her own values. At some point in the lesson, you may wish to add your own positive answer and why you believe that. Students are generally curious about teachers and are interested in a teacher's passion for something noble/good/true. When this is done, resistance does fade, and the student's natural qualities begin to emerge.

# Symbols Used Throughout the Lessons

 This denotes sharing and discussing.

 Read a story.

 Sing a song.

 Artistic expression activity.

 Action-oriented activity.

Teacher note or teacher preparation.

 Quietly Being exercise.

# Educators–Share with the World!

Adults and children using LVEP are invited to share their experiences. You may share your activities and expertise with other educators around the world through the Living Values web site. Visit *www.livingvalues.net*. Or send in your contribution to the nearest LVEP country coordinator.

Annual Evaluation: An important part of any program is evaluation. Your evaluation of the program and observations about changes with children are very important. Kindly let the LVEP coordinator in your country know you are using LVEP, and you will be sent an Educator Evaluation Form annually. Or you may fill out this form on the Web site.

We hope you enjoy *Living Values*. Thank you.

# ONE

# Peace Unit

# 1. PEACE UNIT

Reflection Points . . . . . . . . . . . . . . . . . . . . . . . . . . . . 4

Objectives . . . . . . . . . . . . . . . . . . . . . . . . . . . . . . 4

**PEACE LESSONS**

Lesson 1    Imagining a Peaceful World . . . . . . . . . . . 6

Song    I Am a Peaceful Star . . . . . . . . . . . . . . . . 8

Lesson 2    The Star Story . . . . . . . . . . . . . . . . . . 8

Lesson 3    Stars . . . . . . . . . . . . . . . . . . . . . . . 10

Quietly Being    Peace Star Exercise . . . . . . . . . . . . . . . 10

Lesson 4    Peace Puppets . . . . . . . . . . . . . . . . . . 11

Song    Something Kind . . . . . . . . . . . . . . . . . . 13

Lesson 5    Playing with Peace Puppets . . . . . . . . . . 14

Lesson 6    Paint Peace . . . . . . . . . . . . . . . . . . . 15

Lesson 7    Enact the Star Story . . . . . . . . . . . . . . 16

Lesson 8    Symbols of Peace . . . . . . . . . . . . . . . . 16

Lesson 9    Story . . . . . . . . . . . . . . . . . . . . . . . 17

Lesson 10    Arms Are for Hugging . . . . . . . . . . . . . 17

Lesson 11    Arms Are for Hugging Continues . . . . . . . 18

Teacher Notes    Putting Conflict Resolution into Practice . . . 19

Peace

Lesson 12   Conflict Resolution . . . . . . . . . . . . . . . . . . 21

Song   Monster . . . . . . . . . . . . . . . . . . . . . . 23

Lesson 13   Feelings . . . . . . . . . . . . . . . . . . . . . . 24

Lesson 14   Conflict Resolution Posters . . . . . . . . . . . 25

Lesson 15   Conflict Resolution Posters . . . . . . . . . . . 26

Lesson 16   Animal Peace Masks . . . . . . . . . . . . . . . . 26

Lesson 17   Story . . . . . . . . . . . . . . . . . . . . . . . . 27

Lesson 18   Peaceful World Pictures . . . . . . . . . . . . . 27

Lesson 19   Peaceful World Pictures . . . . . . . . . . . . . 28

Lesson 20   Dove Game . . . . . . . . . . . . . . . . . . . . 28

Lesson 21   Play the Dove Game . . . . . . . . . . . . . . . 30

Lesson 22   Celebrate Peace . . . . . . . . . . . . . . . . . . 30

## Peace Reflection Points

♦ Peace is being quiet inside.

♦ Peace is having good feelings inside.

♦ Peace is when people get along and don't argue or hit.

♦ Peace is having positive thoughts about myself and others.

♦ Peace begins within each one of us.

## Peace Unit

### GOAL: To increase the experience of peace.

### OBJECTIVES:

❑ To enable children to quiet down easily, cooperating with a quiet signal within one minute.

❑ To enable children to enjoy being quiet and peaceful.

❑ To help children increase their ability to concentrate.

❑ To express peace artistically.

❑ To sing a song about peace.

Peace

**GOAL: To increase knowledge about peace.**

**OBJECTIVES:**

❏ To imagine a peaceful world and be able to communicate through words and/or drawing what it would look and feel like.

❏ To play with puppets, enacting peaceful interactions.

❏ To be able to talk about one or more Peace Points.

**GOAL: To build conflict resolution skills.**

**OBJECTIVES:**

❏ For children who are able to verbalize complete sentences to say the phrase: "Arms are for hugging, not for shoving."

❏ To be able to listen to others during a conflict resolution exercise and repeat key phrases of what they say.

❏ To identify through words and/or drawings what they do and do not like others to do.

❏ To identify through words and/or drawings kind things they can do.

# Peace Lessons

Peace Reflection Points can be used to help define this value. They are often used as the first focus during values time or can be a discussion point as part of language arts. Ask the children to share their thoughts and experiences. With very young children, the teacher may wish to use a hand puppet to share the Peace Points.

Peace

For five- through seven-year-olds, the teacher can choose to use some of the words and sentences as content for reading, spelling and writing. As the students continue with the unit, they can create their own Peace Reflection Points. They can draw or write the points or make up short stories about them.

Lesson
1

PEACE LESSON 1

# Imagining a Peaceful World

Peace is often the first value introduced in a school or classroom. If the entire school is supporting a values program, there already may have been an assembly on peace. To reinforce what was said in the assembly, or to introduce in the classroom the first lesson on peace, the teacher may wish to play a song about peace or play peaceful but happy music as the students enter.

**Explain:** "In the next four weeks (or whatever length of time), we're going to learn about something very important. We will learn about peace."

## Discuss/Share

- Who can tell me about peace?
- What is peace?
- What does it mean to have a peaceful world?

Say, "Wonderful answers." Acknowledge all responses and thank the children for sharing. Continue with Imagining a Peaceful World exercise.

Peace

## Imagining a Peaceful World

Lead the children in this imagining exercise. Say the following, pausing at the dots:

"Each one of you is smart. An interesting thing about children is that each child already knows about peace. Today, you can use your imagination to make a picture of a peaceful world in your mind. But to do that you have to be very still for a few minutes. Let your body be comfortable and very still. . . . Imagine a world in which all the people in all the towns of the world like each other and get along very well. There is only peace. And imagine in one of those towns a pretty garden, with trees and flowers. . . . It's very nice in the garden, the grass is soft and you can hear birds singing. . . . You watch the birds fly slowly across the sky. . . . There is a safe and peaceful feeling here. . . . There is a little pond nearby with golden fish swimming slowly. . . . You watch the fish. . . . They are swimming slowly and peacefully. . . . Now, in your mind, picture a swing (or a hammock; whatever the children are familiar with). . . . You sit on the swing. . . . Now one of your favorite people comes up a path, and is happy to see you. . . . That person is very peaceful today . . . and that person slowly pushes you on the swing. . . . You enjoy watching the pretty garden from up high. . . . When you get off the swing, feeling peaceful and full inside, you see yourself in this room. . . ."

## Discuss/Share

Ask the children to share their experiences. Acknowledge their responses.

Peace

### Activity

Ask the children to draw what they imagined.

# Sing a Peace Song

There are many children's songs about peace in different languages around the world. Pick one of your favorites to teach the children. Or make up a song with a simple tune and words, such as the one below. Children really enjoy singing. Sing a peace song every day.

### Song

#### I Am a Peaceful Star

I am a peaceful star, I am,
I am a peaceful star, I am,
When we care together,
When we share together,
We are peaceful stars, we are! *(Repeat)*

Lesson
2

PEACE LESSON 2

## The Star Story

**Teacher Preparation:** If you are working with three- to five-year olds, make a Peace Star out of blue- or rose-colored paper. (Use thick paper, or glue several pieces together so it is thicker.) Sprinkle the star with glitter, or decorate it in any way you wish. With young children you may want to put in facial features and use the Peace Star as a puppet to say the Peace Point.

Begin with the peace song the class sang in Lesson 1.

**Introduction:** Say, "Stars are so beautiful in the sky. They sparkle and shine. They can be seen, but we cannot hear them. They are so quiet and peaceful. One of the ways we can feel peace inside is to think of the stars and imagine ourselves to be just like them. But before we do that, I am going to read you 'The Star Story.'"

## Read

"The Star Story" (Appendix).

When finished reading, say:

"Okay, for a few moments, let's become like the Peace Stars. . . . Relax your body and sit quietly. . . . Sit so quietly that the little star inside of you can shine brightly. . . . It's a very quiet and lovely little star. . . . Shining its light and bringing silence and love into this room. . . . Good."

## Discuss/Share

"The Star Story" and the following Peace Reflection Point: One of the meanings of peace is having good feelings inside. Ask:

- Who can tell me about a Peace Star that had good feelings inside?
- Can anyone give me another example?

## Activity

Ask the children to draw a picture about "The Star Story." The six- and seven-year-olds can add a couple of sentences about their picture.

Peace

PEACE LESSON 3

# Stars

## Discuss/Share

Say, "One of the Peace Reflection Points is 'Peace is feeling quiet inside.' Can someone tell me what that means?" Acknowledge all answers.

Introduction to the Peace Star exercise: Say, "One way to be peaceful is to be quiet inside. Today, let's practice feeling peaceful a little more. . . . One of the ways we can feel peace inside is to think of the stars and imagine ourselves to be just like them. They are so beautiful in the sky, and they sparkle and shine. They can be seen, but we cannot hear them. They are so quiet and peaceful. Let's practice being peaceful. I want everyone to be very still. . . ."

## Peace Star Exercise

"For a few moments, think of the stars and imagine yourselves to be like them . . . quiet and peaceful. . . . Let the body be still. . . . Relax your toes and legs. . . . Relax your stomach . . . and your shoulders. . . . Relax your arms . . . and your face. . . . You are a Peace Star. . . . What color of peace do you shine with today? . . . Perhaps with a rose color that has a feeling of being safe and loved. . . . Perhaps a blue color that shines a light of peace and courage. . . . We are Peace Stars . . . still . . . full . . . relaxed and peaceful. . . . Whenever you want to feel peaceful inside, you can become very still and quiet inside and remember that you are a Peace Star."

---

NOTE TO TEACHER

The Peace Star exercise can also be found in the Appendix.

## Activity

Ask each child to make a star. If they are toddlers, you may wish to cut out the stars beforehand. Or six-year-olds can help the younger children cut them out. Print the first name of each child inside his or her star. (If this is a new class, you can use these as name tags for the next few days.) Ask the children to decorate the stars with the materials available.

End with a peace song.

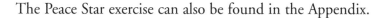

PEACE LESSON 4

# Peace Puppets

Lesson

4

Begin with a peace song.

## Imagining Peaceful Children in a Peaceful World

Lead the children in this imagining exercise. Say the following, pausing at the dots:

"Today, you can use your imagination to make a picture of a peaceful world in your mind. Let your body be comfortable and very still. . . . Imagine a pretty garden, with trees and flowers. . . . It's very nice in the garden, the grass is soft and you can hear birds singing. . . . You watch the birds fly slowly across the sky. . . . There is a safe and peaceful feeling here. . . . There is a little pond nearby

Peace

with golden fish swimming slowly. . . . As you walk by the pond, you see a couple of children your age walking toward you. They wave and say hello. . . . The children invite you to play. . . . You picture yourself playing with them. What game do you play?. . . You play for a while and talk for a while. . . . You see other children playing a game nearby, and everyone is happy. No one fights in this place. . . . You continue to have a good time with your friends. . . . And when it is time to go, you all say goodbye. . . . And then you bring your imagination back here to our classroom."

## Discuss/Share

- What was the peaceful world like that you imagined?
- How did the children act?
- What kind of things did they say?
- What game did you play?
- How did the other children get along?

## Activity

Make Peace Puppets. Start to make Peace Puppets with the children. (You can plan to finish them during the next lesson if you wish.) Tell the children they are making Peace Puppets so the puppets can act out the peaceful world they imagined. Finger or hand puppets can be simple. They can be made with a little envelope of paper or cloth that fits over a finger or the hand. A face can be drawn at the top. Or the children can draw a face on a little piece of paper cut in a circle and then pasted on a stick. Or more elaborate ones can be made, adding yarn as hair and tiny paper circles or buttons for eyes.

## Song

### Something Kind

Chorus:     <sup>Bb</sup>Can you find the time
to be a little <sup>F</sup>kind?
It all comes <sup>Bb</sup>back to you
<sup>Eb</sup>When you <sup>F</sup>do something kind.

Verse:     <sup>Bb</sup>Share a toy <sup>Bb</sup>or some food.
<sup>F</sup>Inside you'll <sup>Bb</sup>feel so good.
<sup>Eb</sup>Remember to <sup>Bb</sup>hold the door.
<sup>F</sup>People will like you <sup>Bb</sup>more.
<sup>Bb</sup>Draw a picture <sup>Bb</sup>for someone.
<sup>F</sup>Being kind is <sup>Bb</sup>so much fun.
<sup>Bb</sup>Go out of your <sup>Bb</sup>way to say,
<sup>F</sup>"How are you today?"

*(Repeat Chorus)*

<sup>Bb</sup>If a friend's <sup>Bb</sup>about to cry,
<sup>F</sup>You might stop <sup>Bb</sup>and ask why.
<sup>Bb</sup>Let him talk <sup>Bb</sup>it all out,
<sup>F</sup>That's what being kind's <sup>Bb</sup>about.
<sup>Bb</sup>It won't cost <sup>Bb</sup>anything,
But <sup>F</sup>being kind will <sup>Bb</sup>always bring
<sup>Bb</sup>A happy smile on <sup>Bb</sup>your face.
<sup>F</sup>You'll make the world a better place.

*(Repeat chorus two times.)*

*(Say)* So remind everyone. Be kind.

*—Contributed by Max and Marcia Nass*

Peace

### PEACE LESSON 5

# Playing with Peace Puppets

Discuss the following Peace Point: Peace is having positive thoughts about myself and others.

- What does that mean?
- What would Peace Puppets say?
- What do Peace Puppets do?
- What would they not do?

## Activity

Finish making the Peace Puppets. The teacher may want to demonstrate for the class with a Peace Puppet on each hand. Allow time for the children to play with their Peace Puppets. At sharing time, ask small groups of three or four children to stand together in front of the class and allow their finger puppets to interact. The teacher can ask the puppets questions about what they like to do. Perhaps the teacher's Peace Puppet can interact with the children's Peace Puppets. Continue to involve the puppets in conversation. Maybe the Peace Puppets would like to put on a play.

End the lesson with a peace song.

Peace

PEACE LESSON 6

# Paint Peace

Lead the children in the Peace Star exercise from Lesson 3.

## Discuss/Share

- What does being quiet feel like?
- When do you feel most peaceful?
- If peace were a color, what color would it be for you?

Positively acknowledge all answers.

## Activity

Provide finger paints and ask the children to paint peace. The teacher may wish to play relaxing, peaceful music as the children paint.

End with a peace song or two.

---

NOTE TO TEACHER

Putting Peace into Practice: When you want the children to pause quietly, hold up the Peace Star or say, "For a minute, let's be as peaceful and full of quiet happiness as the stars. . . ." This can be done several times during the day if you like. Wait until they are quiet—and a few moments longer so they can become peaceful—then affirm their good efforts, saying quietly, "You are Peace Stars."

Sometimes three- and four-year-olds like to hug the Peace Star during the day. They can hug the one made as an example just before the teacher reads "The Star Story," or a Star Pillow can be made.

---

# Enact the Star Story

Tell "The Star Story" again, asking comprehension questions afterward.

## Activity

Allow the children to act out "The Star Story" using stars they have made previously as props. Assign roles, and ask the children to act out the story as the teacher slowly reads it again. Or with very little children, tell them to pretend to be a star from "The Star Story" and let them create a "Peace Star Dance," creating peaceful movements as the teacher plays peaceful music.

# Symbols of Peace

Discuss what represents peace to the children: Say, "Today I want you to think of something that means peace to you. Perhaps it's a star, a dove, a cookie, a cat, a lake, or . . . ?"

## Activity

Instruct the children to draw an object that means peace to them. When they are finished, the teacher can allow the students to take turns in front of a projector light or a lantern, moving their object in front of the light in a darkened room, and telling why it is something that means peace for them.

*—Adapted from an activity by Dominique Ache*

Ask the students to decide if they would like to hang the objects from the ceiling (or whatever is convenient for the setting).

---

PEACE LESSON 9

# Story

Tell a story about peace that is one of your favorites, or one that is from the culture of the children.

Discuss the story and have them draw a picture about it or act it out as you tell it again.

---

PEACE LESSON 10

# Arms Are for Hugging

Begin the session with a peace song.

Discuss the following Peace Point: Peace is when people get along and don't argue or hit.

Root Sentence: Ask each child to finish the sentence: "In a peaceful world, _____." The teacher can start by explaining what they will be doing and giving a few examples. Include the example, "In a peaceful world, arms are used for hugging."

*Peace*

Then ask each child to finish the sentence: "In a peaceful world, there would not be . . ." Ask:

- How do you feel when you are hugged or spoken to sweetly?
- How do you feel when you are shoved, pushed or hit?

Introduce the phrase: In peace, arms are used for hugging, not for shoving. Ask the children, "What are arms used for?" . . . (Hugging) "That's right, hugging." Ask them to repeat the phrase, "Arms are for hugging" or "Arms are for giving, not for grabbing."

The teacher can give everyone a hug and/or ask the children to give each other a hug. (In some countries, it is important to ensure that girls hug girls and boys hug boys.)

## Activity

Tell the children they can draw a picture about the things discussed today.

End with a peace song.

PEACE LESSON 11

# Arms Are for Hugging Continues

Begin the session with a song.

Root Sentence: Ask the children to stand in a circle, and tell them that today you would like to hear more of their ideas about a peaceful world. You would like them to finish the same sentence they used the day before: "In a peaceful world, _____

_____."

Peace

Review the saying: "Arms are for hugging," and then the longer sentence, "Arms are for hugging, not for shoving." Lead the children in saying these two sentences.

**Explain** that an important part of peace is knowing when to say "no." When someone is hurting you, it is a good idea to let that person know you do not like that and want him or her to stop. Tell the children they can say, "I don't like it when you do that. Arms are for hugging, not for shoving." Lead them in repeating the sentences.

## Activity

Instruct the children to write the word "PEACE" in large letters on colored paper and to decorate it with pictures of flowers or whatever they wish. For younger children, lightly draw the letter "P" or the word "PEACE" and ask them to trace it and then decorate it.

TEACHER NOTE PRIOR TO LESSON 12

### Putting Conflict Resolution into Practice

If the adult observes one child pushing another, firmly but patiently say:

"Tell him or her what you don't like. Say, 'I don't like it when you hit me. Arms are for hugging, not for shoving.'"

If you encourage the children to use this phrase, they will soon be able to apply it independently. Conflicts will decrease as their appropriate communication skills develop.

If there is a more serious conflict, ask both children to sit down.

Ask one child to say how he or she feels while the other listens. Ask the second child, "What did he or she say?" After it is repeated, ask that child the same question (how he or she feels) and have the first child repeat that.

Then ask each one to tell the other what he or she would like the other not to do. Ask the listener to repeat what the speaker says.

Then ask them each to say what they would like the other to do. Each listener is to repeat what the speaker says.

Ask if they can do that for a certain amount of time. Set a short enough time so they will be successful. For very young children, ask, "Can you do that while you play with the blocks?" Or, "Can you do that until recess or break?"

Praise them for playing peacefully when they have been doing that.

In the above interaction, it is important for the adult to encourage the children to speak directly to one another and repeat what the other says. As each child voices her or his feelings, the intensity will decrease automatically as each child repeats how the other feels and the teacher listens, too. As the adult, do not adopt the position of "judge." Comments that criticize, moralize and judge decrease the effectiveness of the above process. One of the purposes of the process is for the children to learn to communicate and come up with appropriate solutions.

## Summarizing the Steps of Conflict Resolution:

The teacher questions each of the two children, asking the children to listen when the other speaks so he or she can repeat what was said.

Questions to each child:

How do you feel?                          What did he or she say?
                                                      *(Repeat)*

What would you like                       What did he or she say?
   *(name of child)* not to do?            *(Repeat)*

What would you like _____               What did he or she say?
   to do?                                         *(Repeat)*

Can you both do that?

*(Set a short amount of time for them to do that, and praise them both at the end of that time for doing that.)*

---

PEACE LESSON 12

# Conflict Resolution

Lesson 12

**Practice:** Ask students to repeat the sentences they learned last time.

- Arms are for hugging.
- Arms are for hugging, not for shoving.

And when someone uses their arms to hurt, they can say:

- I don't like it when you do that. Arms are for hugging, not for shoving.

Peace

Ask children to practice the above line several times, encouraging them to say it clearly and firmly.

**Explain:**

- Sometimes it is important to talk to people when we feel sad, angry or upset. If someone has a problem with someone else, that child can talk to the teacher or the teacher's helper, and often the adult will help the child resolve the problem with the other child.
- When we talk to each other, then we understand each other, and we can solve the problem.
- When there is a problem, three questions help:

  How do you feel?

  What would you like the other person not to do?

  What would you like the other person to do?

## Discuss/Share

Post the first question on the board: How do you feel? Ask:

- How do you feel when someone hits you?
- How do you feel when someone calls you a name?
- What else don't you like other students to do?
- How do you feel when they do that?

Listen and acknowledge their responses. As they give you their answers, the teacher may wish to draw a sad face by the question or an angry face, etc.

Post the second question: What would you like the other person not to do? Repeat what they have already told you they don't like during the last set of questions. Ask:

- Is there anything else you don't like other students to do?

Post the third question: What would you like the other person to do? Ask:

- What do you like other students to do instead?
- What are friendly things you can do?
- What are kind things people can do?
- What are peaceful things people can do?

Thank them for their answers.

**Demonstrate** Conflict Resolution: Ask two students to volunteer to enact a "pretend" problem-solving demonstration. Explain the process—that each student will be asked the same questions. Each student needs to listen carefully so he or she can repeat what the other student said. Model the process, asking the three questions and asking each child to repeat the other person's answer. (See Summarizing the Steps of Conflict Resolution on the prior page.)

# Song

### Monster

| | |
|---|---|
| Chorus: | ᴬI don't want to be a monster. |
| | I want peace today. |
| | I don't want to be a monster. |
| | Monster go away! |
| Verse: | ᴬWhen the monster comes out, |
| | ᴮ ᵐⁱⁿI scream and shout. |
| | ᴰHow can I make it go a-ᴬway? |
| | If I cool off awhile, |
| | And ᴮ ᵐⁱⁿput on a smile, |

Peace

ᴰSoon everything will be o-ᴬkay.

The monster in me

Is ᴮ ᵐⁱⁿalways angry,

ᴰIt wants to fight and never ᴬcares.

So I give myself a hug.

ᴮ ᵐⁱⁿOut comes the love.

And the monster disap-ᴬpears.

*(Repeat chorus two times.)*

*—Contributed by Max and Marcia Nass*

---

**Lesson**
**13**

PEACE LESSON 13

# Feelings

Discuss the following Peace Reflection Point: Peace is having good feelings inside. Then ask:

- How do you feel when another child calls you names?
- How do you feel when another child says something nice to you?
- What do you feel when someone does something kind?
- What kind things do you like others to do?
- What kind things do you like to do?

Lead the children in the Peace Star exercise.

## Activity

Ask the children to work in groups of two. Ask each pair of children to draw one picture about the kind things the children like to do and like others to do.

Peace

PEACE LESSON 14

# Conflict Resolution Posters

**Review** the sentence to use when a child is stopping a conflict with another child who is pushing or shoving:

- I don't like it when you do that. Arms are for hugging, not for shoving.

Review the three things we talk about if there is a conflict:

- How do you feel?
- What would you like the other person not to do?
- What would you like the other person to do?

Discuss all three questions with the students as was done in Lesson 13. But this time make a list of all their answers.

## Activity

For little children, ask them to draw a picture about the things they want other people to do instead of fight. For six- and seven-year olds, ask them to form small groups. Each small group can make a poster of things the children do not want other people to do, and then a poster of the things they want other people to do instead. Ask them to create one poster now and the second poster during Lesson 15.

End with a peace song. You may wish to enjoy moving in a circle at the same time.

Peace

## PEACE LESSON 15
# Conflict Resolution Posters

Begin with a peace song.

## Activity

Finish the posters from Lesson 14. Then ask each group of children to share its posters (or drawings) with the whole class.

Demonstrate conflict resolution with two student volunteers, as was done in Lesson 13.

End with the Peace Star exercise from Lesson 3.

## PEACE LESSON 16
# Animal Peace Masks

## Activity

Tell the children that today they can make a mask of an animal (or a drawing if that is more appropriate for your culture). Think of why that animal would like peace.

Root Sentence: After the children make their mask or drawing, they can share: "I am a _____, and I like peace because _____."

End with a peace song, or the children can dance a dance of peace with their masks on. Each animal is to be peaceful with the other animals.

Peace

PEACE LESSON 17

# Story

Begin with a peace song.

## Activity

Tell another story about peace from your culture or the culture(s) of the children.

Discuss it afterward, and then do an artistic or expressive activity.

PEACE LESSON 18

# Peaceful World Pictures

**Imagining exercise:** Do the Imagining a Peaceful World exercise in Lesson 4.

## Discuss/Share

Ask the children what they imagined and about their feelings during the imagination exercise.

## Activity

Divide the children into small groups and allow each small group to draw or paint a picture of a peaceful world on a large piece of paper. Play relaxing music and ask the children to enjoy feeling peaceful as they make the big pictures. These may take a couple of days to finish.

End with a peace song.

Peace

**Lesson 19**

PEACE LESSON 19

# Peaceful World Pictures

Begin with a peace song.

Discuss the following Peace Reflection Point: Peace is having positive thoughts about myself and others.

## Activity

Allow each group to continue working on its large picture. The children may wish to attach some of the things they have made previously during the unit on peace.

**Lesson 20**

PEACE LESSON 20

# Dove Game

Begin with a peace song.

Discuss the following Peace Reflection Point: Peace begins within each one of us.

## Activity

Make squares for the Dove Game or for an adaptation of a children's board game in your country. While a board game will be too complex for many three- and four-year olds, they would enjoy making the squares.

The Dove Game is an adaptation of a game from Spain called the Goose Game. The Spanish board game has squares that form a spiral. Small groups of children can make the board game, drawing objects on small pieces of paper that can later be pasted onto a larger piece of paper in the form of a spiral. Or each member of the entire class can make one square, and then the squares can be laid on the floor of the classroom or outside in a large spiral. In the former, children would use dice and markers when they play. In the latter, they would use dice, but then stand by the square on the ground as they advance toward the finish.

## Discuss/Share

Ask the children to think about what pictures they would like to make for their game. There should be doves and other symbols of peace. One out of every five pictures should be a dove. Two out of every five pictures can be something that disrupts peace. For these, ask the children to draw pictures about what things they do not like other children to do. Arrange the pictures so that the fifth square is a dove, and then the tenth, fifteenth, twentieth, etc. The last picture should be a picture of a completely peaceful world.

**Game Rules:** To play, the child rolls the dice. When a child lands on a picture of a dove, he or she says, "Dove to dove, I fly above," and then moves to the next dove (five spaces up). If a child lands on a disrupting-peace square, he or she is to give a solution. For example, if it is a picture of someone calling a name, the child can say, "I don't like it when you do that; I want you to stop." Or, if it is a picture of someone hitting another, she can say, "Arms are for hugging, not for shoving." When a child thinks of a solution, the child advances to the next peace square. The game is over when everyone reaches the last square of a peaceful world. Allow the children to encourage and help each

Peace

other. The teacher can lead the applause when all the children reach the last square.

*—Adapted from an activity contributed by Encarnación Royo Costa*

**Lesson 21**

PEACE LESSON 21

# Play the Dove Game

Begin with the Peaceful Star exercise (Lesson 3).

## Activity

Play the Dove Game that the children made in the previous lesson. First explain the rules, then ask the children to practice verbal responses for landing on the dove and the conflict squares. Then ask them to play the game.

End with a peace song.

**Lesson 22**

PEACE LESSON 22

# Celebrate Peace

Begin with a peace song.

Discuss all the things you have done and what you have learned during your peace time. Admire all your work around the room.

Do the Peaceful Star exercise.

Do a peace dance or play the peace game the class created.

End with a peace song. Perhaps share cookies or sweets in the form of stars.

# TWO

# Respect Unit

# 2. RESPECT UNIT

Reflection Points. . . . . . . . . . . . . . . . . . . . . . . . . 34

Objectives . . . . . . . . . . . . . . . . . . . . . . . . . . . . . 34

**RESPECT LESSONS**

Lesson 1   Mirror, Mirror . . . . . . . . . . . . . . . . . . . 36

Lesson 2   My Hands. . . . . . . . . . . . . . . . . . . . . . . 37

Lesson 3   My Hands Song. . . . . . . . . . . . . . . . . . . . 38

Quietly Being   Respect Star Exercise . . . . . . . . . . . . . 40

Lesson 4   My Qualities . . . and Their Echo. . . . . . . . 40

Song   Each One of Us Is Beautiful . . . . . . . . . . . 42

Lesson 5   Lily the Leopard . . . . . . . . . . . . . . . . . . 43

Lesson 6   My Qualities Picture. . . . . . . . . . . . . . . . 44

Lesson 7   Me Silhouettes. . . . . . . . . . . . . . . . . . . 45

Lesson 8   Me Silhouettes. . . . . . . . . . . . . . . . . . . 46

Lesson 9   Knowing Me Necklace. . . . . . . . . . . . . . . . 46

Lesson 10   Knowing Me Necklace . . . . . . . . . . . . . . . 46

Song   In Your Shoes . . . . . . . . . . . . . . . . . . . 47

Lesson 11   Giving Respect at School . . . . . . . . . . . . 48

Lesson 12   Giving Respect at Home. . . . . . . . . . . . . . 49

Respect

Lesson 13   Play Microphone . . . . . . . . . . . . . . . . . . . 50

Lesson 14   You're Wonderful, Too! . . . . . . . . . . . . . . 51

Song   Nice Words . . . . . . . . . . . . . . . . . . . . . 51

Lesson 15   Telling a Story About Respect . . . . . . . . . . 52

Lesson 16   Telling a Story About Respect . . . . . . . . . . 52

Lesson 17   Greetings of the World . . . . . . . . . . . . . . . 53

Lesson 18   Conflict-Ending Social Skill . . . . . . . . . . . 54

Lesson 19   Conflict Resolution with Respect . . . . . . . . 55

Lesson 20   Story or Painting . . . . . . . . . . . . . . . . . . 56

Lesson 21   What I'm Proud Of . . . . . . . . . . . . . . . . . 56

Lesson 22   Crowns . . . . . . . . . . . . . . . . . . . . . . . . . 57

Sequence of Activities After the Peace
and Respect Units . . . . . . . . . . . . . . . . . . 58

## Respect Reflection Points

♦ Respect is feeling good about myself.

♦ Respect is knowing I am unique and valuable.

♦ Respect is valuing myself.

♦ Respect is knowing I am lovable and capable.

♦ Respect is liking who I am.

♦ Respect is listening to others.

♦ Respect is knowing others are valuable, too.

♦ Respect is treating others nicely.

## Respect Unit

**GOAL: To increase the experience of self-respect.**
**OBJECTIVES:**

❏ To state something good that they do with their hands.

Respect

❑ To enjoy the Respect Star exercise, as demonstrated by sitting quietly during it and appearing happy to do so.

❑ To identify the self as lovable and capable.

❑ For each child to name two or more positive qualities about himself or herself.

**GOAL: To increase knowledge about respect.**

**OBJECTIVES:**

❑ To be able to talk about one or more Respect Points.

❑ To share a story about respect through words or a picture.

**GOAL: To build respectful relationship skills.**

**OBJECTIVES:**

❑ To tell a classmate one or two positive qualities the child sees in him or her.

❑ To give respect to others by listening to others when they are speaking, as demonstrated by being able to listen to others during the values discussion time.

❑ To identify and make a picture of nice behaviors toward others.

❑ To speak with respect to teachers and peers during conflict resolution exercises.

# Respect Lessons

Respect Reflection Points can be used to help define the value. They are often used as the first focus during values time or can be a discussion point as part of language arts. Ask the children to share their thoughts and experiences. With very young children,

Respect

the teacher may wish to use a hand puppet to share the Respect Points. It is a perfect time to positively reinforce listening, as one of the definitions used for respect is listening to others.

For five- through seven-year-olds, the teacher may choose to use some of the words and sentences as content for reading, spelling and writing. As the students continue with the unit, they can create their own Respect Points. They can then draw or write those or make up short stories.

**Lesson 1**

RESPECT LESSON 1

# Mirror, Mirror

Discuss the following Respect Reflection Points:

♦ Respect is knowing I am unique and valuable. (The teacher will need to define the words unique—one of a kind; you are the only you—and valuable.)

♦ Respect is knowing I am lovable and capable.

**Teacher Preparation:** Place a mirror in a corner of the room with a curtain around it.

**Mirror, Mirror Activity:** Tell the children there is someone very special they can see. The child they will see is sweet and strong and loved. This child is unique and very valuable. Tell the children they can meet this person.

Tell the children you want them not to tell each other about who they saw behind the curtain until everyone has had the chance to see. If there is only a small group of children, wait until each child has had a turn to look behind the curtain.

Respect

## Discuss

Listen to their reaction about seeing their own reflection in the mirror. Repeat the Respect Reflection Points that each one is unique and valuable, and respect is knowing I am lovable and capable.

*—Contributed by Dominique Ache*

## Activity

Arrange for each child to make a star with his or her name on it and the words *lovable* and *capable*. They can cut, color and decorate their stars. Use materials that are available—perhaps some glitter.

---

RESPECT LESSON 2

# My Hands

Lesson
2

Discuss the following Respect Reflection Point: Respect is feeling good about myself. Ask:

• When do you feel good about yourself?

Children will often mention specific things they do that are helpful to others as a time when they feel good about themselves. Confirm that when we do good things, we feel good about ourselves. They may mention that they feel good about themselves when they feel peaceful. Acknowledge their responses.

Respect

## Activity

In this activity, each child does hand prints of both hands. Ask the children to make their own hand prints. They can paint their own hand and make the print with the help of the teacher, or the teacher can help the youngest children with both. Cut out the hands. Ask them to arrange the cut-out hands in a circle on a large sheet of paper. These can be stuck down with paste, and their name written nearby.

## Discuss/Share

In a circle or with the children sitting in a group, the teacher can talk about the activity and draw the children's attention to the reality of hands doing actions that create good or hands doing actions that create sorrow, e.g., hitting or pinching others. Ask every child what nice things or what good actions they would like their hands to do.

Write down their answers within the circle of cut-out hands.

Lesson
3

RESPECT LESSON 3

# My Hands Song

## Activity

Make up a simple song or poem using the words written from the My Hands activity of the previous lesson. Have a good time, making hand movements to go with the words of the song.

Respect

The following song was created by children in a nursery in London.

### These Little Hands

These little hands, what can they do?

They can paint a picture for Mummy and for you.

These little hands, what can they do?

They can hug you and show I love you.

These little hands, what can they do?

They can play the drums one and two.

These little hands, what can they do?

They can blow a kiss to show I love you.

These little hands, what can they do?

They can gently stroke your cheek and wave hello.

## Activity

Today the children can make a card for their parents. Cut out a heart from colored cards. The smaller children can trace both of their hands on the heart and color them. The older children can trace their hands on white paper, cut them out and paste them on the heart. For the smaller children, write the following on the back with felt tips: My little hands do good things. They _____ (Write out the child's answer.) For the five-year-olds, the teacher could preprint the words with pencil and the children could write over the lines with felt-tip pins.

Do the following Respect Star exercise.

**Introduction:** Say: "We've been singing about some of the good things that you do. Doing good things helps us respect ourselves. It is also important to know what we were talking about the other

*Respect*

day—that each one of us is unique and valuable, and lovable and capable. Filling yourself up with these feelings is what respect feels like inside. Let's have the Respect Star join us Peaceful Stars."

## Respect Star Exercise

"For a few moments, be very still. . . . Relax your toes and legs. . . . Relax your stomach . . . and your shoulders. . . . Relax your arms . . . and your face. . . . The Respect Star knows each person brings special qualities to the world. . . . You are a beautiful little star . . . you are lovable and capable . . . you are who you are. . . . You are unique and valuable. . . . Enjoy the feeling of respect inside. . . . You are stars of peace that are lovable and capable. . . . Let yourself be quiet and peaceful inside. . . . Whenever you want to feel especially good inside, be very still inside and remember that you are a star full of peace, a star full of respect."

---

NOTE TO TEACHER

The Respect Star exercise can also be found in the Appendix.

---

Lesson
4

RESPECT LESSON 4

# My Qualities . . . and Their Echo

## Discuss/Share

Say, "Today I want you to name some of the things that you like about yourself." Ask:

Respect

- Can anyone tell me some good words your mom or dad (grandparents, foster parents, caregivers) use to describe you, or words that we've used in here?
- We used the words lovable and capable. What other words can you think of? . . . smart, nice, funny, polite . . . That's very good. Let's list all the words we can think of to describe ourselves or others.

You may want to add a few to their list: kind, sweet, gentle, friendly, loving, giving, helpful, a hard worker—helping define them as needed.

Say, "Now, I want each one of you to think of three that are especially yours."

For three-year-olds, you may wish to start with just one quality. Talk about this again the next day, and ask the children to think of a second one. The teacher can then ask everyone to stand in a circle. Each child takes a turn to name his or her three qualities. (Or one or two qualities, depending on the age of the children. If the teacher knows this is a daunting experience for any one child, that child may instead stand by the teacher and tell him or her the qualities. The teacher can then say, "Dana is . . .") After the child or teacher has named the qualities, all the children in the circle are to repeat what was said together: "Dana is . . ." This can be a powerful, positive experience. The teacher can praise the children for showing respect by listening well.

Sing the following song or another song on valuing each one.

Respect

## Each One of Us Is Beautiful

<sup>C</sup>Each one of us is <sup>C</sup>beautiful,

As beautiful as can <sup>G</sup>be

<sup>D</sup>If you can see my <sup>G</sup>beauty

You know <sup>D</sup>how to look at <sup>G</sup>me.

<sup>G</sup>I'm full of love and <sup>C</sup>laughter

I <sup>D</sup>have a smile for <sup>G</sup>you

I'm smart and <sup>C</sup>friendly

You're <sup>D</sup>smart and friendly, <sup>G</sup>too.

<sup>G</sup>Each one of us is <sup>C</sup>beautiful

<sup>D</sup>Like a little <sup>G</sup>star,

I'm so happy <sup>C</sup>we can see

How <sup>D</sup>beautiful we <sup>G</sup>are.

NOTE TO TEACHER

## Affirming Qualities

Of course, regularly reinforcing positive qualities is important and something that most teachers do. It is especially important when a child is first learning to acquire a new skill, such as carefully listening to others. All humans like warm regard, an extra smile and hearing about their positive qualities. While recognition is good to give immediately during the acquisition of a new skill, the adult can also keep a sheet of paper for noting down positive behaviors of the children. Write good things you observe the children saying or doing during the day or week. Share your comments during circle time or sharing time when you have at least one comment for each child. (It is easiest if you have the children's

Respect

names listed in a column already.) Add a quality to each one of the specific behaviors you noted down. For example, "Mario helped Lin when the juice spilled. That was helpful and gave respect to Lin. And Lin used good manners with our new member, Sherry. That was friendly and gave respect to Sherry. Dana remembered to use his arms for hugging. That was being a great model of peace and showed that he has respect for himself. Mohammed listened so well during . . ."

RESPECT LESSON 5

# Lily the Leopard

Lesson

5

Read the "Lily the Leopard" story to the children (Appendix).

## Discuss/Share

The story. Ask,

- Why did Lily feel sad?
- Why did she run away?
- Who did she see when she woke up after her nap?
- Was she surprised to see a leopard with green spots?
- What qualities was Lily able to list about herself? (kind, caring, friendly, loving, brave and strong)
- Was she happy to discover that she had those qualities?
- How do you feel when you think of your qualities?

Respect

## Activity

Draw a picture about the story, "Lily the Leopard."

Sing "Each One of Us Is Beautiful" or another song on respect.

RESPECT LESSON 6

# My Qualities Picture

## Discuss/Share

Who remembers some of the Respect Points we've been talking about? Another Respect Point is: Respect is liking who I am. What does that mean? Who remembers some of the qualities we talked about the other day?

**Circle Activity with Root Sentences:** Ask the children to stand in a circle and hold hands (in cultures where appropriate). Each child in the circle takes a turn, stating two of his or her qualities, starting with "I am _____ and _____."

Do the Respect Star exercise (Lesson 3, Respect unit).

## Activity

Ask each child to draw a picture of himself or herself and write a couple of his or her qualities on the picture. Help the little children write the words. Older ones can write a sentence: I am _____

_____.

RESPECT LESSON 7

# Me Silhouettes

## Discuss/Share

- Do you remember the story we read the other day, "Lily the Leopard?"
- Would you like me to read it again? (Read it again if they wish.)
- What color spots did Lily have?
- What color spots did Lenny have?
- Who remembers what color spots Lucy had?

Note afterward: Lily and Lenny and Lucy were all leopards, but they each had different color spots. Each one of you is a child, but no one looks the same. Respect is knowing each one of us is unique and valuable.

Materials: Large pieces of paper—the size of the children—will be needed, along with crayons or paints. This is a great time to recycle old buttons, yarn or thread.

## Activity

Ask some of the children to lie on the ground on pieces of paper while others draw their silhouette around them. Each child can then cut out his or her shape.

Respect

RESPECT LESSON 8

# Me Silhouettes

Sing "Each One of Us Is Beautiful" or another respect song.

## Activity

Continue to make the Me Silhouettes. The children can draw, paint or color their clothes, hair and features. Each child can share his or her silhouette in front of the class. You may wish to display their art on the walls.

Lessons
9-10

RESPECT LESSONS AND 10

# Knowing Me Necklace

Do the Respect Star exercise (Lesson 3, Respect unit).

## Discuss/Share

Talk with the children about what they like to play, something they like to do at school, something they like to do at home and something they like to eat. In your questions, include a few activities from the children's culture which they are likely to enjoy.

## Activity

On small pieces of paper, make drawings of the activities they like doing and a couple of their favorite things. Join these pieces

*Respect*

of paper together to make a paper necklace to place around the neck of their Me Silhouette.

## Song

### In Your Shoes

Chorus:  $^A$If you could walk in my shoes
$^D$You would see,
$^D$What it feels like $^A$in my shoes
$^D$To be $^A$me.
If I $^A$could walk in your shoes,
$^D$I'd know too.
What it feels like $^A$in your shoes
$^D$To $^E$be $^A$you.

Verse:  $^D$I'd eat chocolate,
And $^A$you'd eat vanilla.
$^D$We'd see how it feels
To $^A$become the other fella.
$^D$I'd live in your house,
And $^A$you'd live in mine.
$^D$We'd understand each $^E$other
In a $^A$very short time.

*(Repeat chorus.)*
$^D$I'd look like you,
And $^A$you'd look like me.
$^D$It would be hard
For $^A$us to be enemies.
$^D$I'd feel your feelings,

Respect

ᴬSo in the end

ᴰWhen we're back in ᴱour own shoes

We'd ᴬend up being friends.

*(Repeat chorus two more times.)*

—*Contributed by Max and Marcia Nass*

Lesson

# 11

RESPECT LESSON 11

# Giving Respect at School

Discuss the following Respect Reflection Point: Respect is treating others nicely. Ask:

- What does that mean?
- What are ways we can treat others nicely at school?
- What are ways you like to be treated by your classmates?
- How do we give respect when we talk to someone?
- What do others do that shows they respect you?

## Activity

Who can show me? Ask the children to demonstrate some ways of treating others with respect. Make it fun—provide contrast by asking them to demonstrate how they do not like to be treated. For example, demonstrate a respectful way to talk to someone and a disrespectful way. Note the tone of voice (pleasant versus angry or whiny) and the facial expression (pleasant versus angry, etc.) Reinforce the positive.

Instruct the children to make a picture of what they have spoken about.

Respect

Sing a respect song and one of the peace songs from the previous unit on peace.

---

RESPECT LESSON 12

# Giving Respect at Home

Do the Respect Star exercise.

## Discuss/Share

- How do we give respect at home?
- How do we give respect when we ask for something? (Saying "please," looking at the other person, if culturally appropriate, etc.)
- How do we give respect when we listen?
- How do we feel when we are listened to?
- What advice would the Respect Star give to the children of the world?
- What advice would the Respect Star give to you if you were older?
- What kind of adult do you want to be?

## Activity

Draw a picture.

Respect

Lesson
# 13

RESPECT LESSON 13
# Play Microphone

## Activity

Make a play microphone with the children.

Discuss the following Respect Point: Respect is listening to others. Ask:

- When children are talking, what do they like others to do?
- How do children feel when others listen?
- How do children feel when others talk over them?

Note: If some of the children complain that others talk over them, explain that part of respect is listening to others.

## Activity

Model introducing themselves, another child or the teacher. Allow the children to take turns introducing each other, practicing giving respect while speaking and giving respect while listening (that is, taking turns listening before speaking). If there is a real microphone available, allow the children to use it after they have practiced with the play microphone.

—*Contributed by Encarnación Royo Costa*

Do the Peace Star exercise.

End with one of the respect songs and perhaps doing a circle dance at the same time.

Respect

RESPECT LESSON 14

# You're Wonderful, Too!

Start with the Respect Star exercise.

## Discuss/Share

Say, "Part of self-respect is knowing the wonderful things about yourself. Today, as we sit in the circle, I want you to think about some of the good things that you know about yourself, like we did the other day. Can anybody tell me some things? . . . Yes, you are lovable, smart . . . you like to do. . . . Now, I want each of you in the circle to take a turn saying one good thing about yourself. You can say, for example, 'I'm smart, or I'm lovable, or I'm helpful.' Okay? Everyone think of one good thing about yourself. Okay, let's go around the circle. . . . Great.

"Once we know some of the wonderful things in us, then it is easy to see the wonderful things in others, too. Respect is knowing that others are valuable, too. Now, I want us to take turns around the circle again, but this time I want you to say something good about the person sitting next to you." (Indicate right or left.)

Learn another respect song. You might want to try the following.

### Nice Words

Chorus:  ᶜI say nice words to you;
You say nice words to me.
ᴳCan you find a nice word
For everyone you ᶜsee?

Respect

ᴳEveryone you ᶜsee?

"You're ᴳfunny."
"You're ᶜhappy"
"You're ᴳalways very ᶜkind."
ᴳNice words make you ᶜfeel good;
ᴰ⁷Say them all the ᴳ⁷time.

ᴳ"You're smart,
I ᑫlike you;
ᴳYou're a friend of ᶜmine."
ᴳNice words make you ᶜfeel good;
ᴰ⁷Say them all the ᴳtime.

*(Repeat chorus two times.)*

—*Contributed by Max and Marcia Nass*

End with the song, "Each One of Us Is Beautiful."

**Lessons 15-16**

RESPECT LESSONS 15 AND 16
# Telling a Story About Respect

## Discuss/Share

Ask the children to think about someone they respect. Why do they respect that person? Perhaps they can remember something special the person did for them or someone else. Perhaps the person did something special to show love to someone, or perhaps they took care of an animal or the earth.

Respect

## Activity

Make a television frame out of cardboard that is big enough for the children to stand behind and look through. Allow the children to share their stories about respect for someone.

*—Contributed by Marcia Maria Lins de Medeiros*

End with the Respect Star exercise.

---

RESPECT LESSON 17

# Greetings of the World

Lesson
17

**Introduction:** One way of showing respect to others is learning about their culture and learning to say hello in their language. Learn about different ways of greeting others with respect around the world. For this age group, perhaps learn to say hello in two to four languages.

## Activity

Learn to say hello in two to four different languages other than your own. Perhaps children in the class have a variety of languages to share. Enjoy practicing.

*—Contributed by Dominique Ache*

## Activity

Play the Dove Game from the Peace unit (Lesson 20), but substitute saying hello in _____ (the different languages

Respect

the children learned) for the conflict squares. The children and the teacher can prepare the squares before starting the game.

**Lesson 18**

RESPECT LESSON 18

# Conflict-Ending Social Skill

Begin with the song "Each One of Us Is Beautiful" or another respect song.

Practice greetings of the world: Say hello to each other in the different languages introduced in Lesson 17.

Discuss the following Respect Reflection Point: Respect is treating others nicely. Ask, "What does that mean?"

Sometimes people do or say things that are not nice. That means that they are not feeling full of respect. Ask:

- What don't you like people to say to you?
- How do you feel when that happens?
- What don't you like people to do?
- How do you feel when that happens?

When someone says something or does something that you don't like, you can say: "I don't like it when you do that. I want you to stop."

Ask the children to say those two sentences several times— saying them firmly, clearly and with self-respect.

Ask for two volunteers, and ask the children to role-play this exercise. Ask several more children to role-play. Ask:

- When do people usually call names? (When someone will not share, etc.)

Respect

• What is something we can do then?

End with the Respect Star exercise.

---

RESPECT LESSON 19

# Conflict Resolution with Respect

Begin with a respect song.

Practice greetings of the world: Say hello to each other in the different languages introduced in Lesson 17.

Practice the conflict-ending social skill: Yesterday we practiced two sentences: "I don't like it when you do that. I want you to stop." Ask:

• When do you use that? ("Yes, that's right. When people call you names or are doing something that you don't like.")

Review conflict resolution skills.

> TEACHER NOTE: PLEASE REFER TO
> LESSON 12 OF THE PEACE UNIT
> TO DO THE FOLLOWING:
>
> Say, "Our three questions for solving a problem when there is a conflict are up here (on a poster or wall). Let's practice them again, but paying attention to listening with respect, and repeating what the other person said with respect."

Respect

Demonstrate the conflict resolution skills with two students, as was done during Lesson 12 of the Peace unit. With seven-year-olds, ask two more students to come up to be peace monitors, and instruct them to ask the three questions. They can practice asking the questions with respect. Positively acknowledge their successes.

End with a peace song.

## RESPECT LESSON 20
# Story or Painting

Read a story from your culture about valuing or respecting someone or something. Then discuss the story and draw it or enact it.

Option: Provide finger paints and suggest to the children that they paint a picture that feels like respect. Begin with the Respect Star exercise.

## RESPECT LESSON 21
# What I'm Proud Of

Discuss the following Respect Reflection Point: Respect is valuing myself.

- When do you value yourself?
- When do you feel proud of yourself?

Listen and acknowledge their responses. Tell them each person is valuable, and it is okay to value themselves because they are valuable.

Respect

## Activity

Ask the children to draw pictures of themselves doing something each one feels good about or is proud of—or just pictures of themselves when they are feeling valuable.

RESPECT LESSON 22

# Crowns

Lesson

# 22

## Activity

Tell the children that today for the ending activity they can make crowns of their qualities. Take a piece of paper wide enough to wrap around a child's head. Draw a crown on it with tabs on each end. Draw triangles and diamonds for jewels on another piece of paper. The adults can write in the qualities that each child identified, if the children are too young to do that for themselves. The children can color the crown and the virtue "jewels" and cut them out. The jewels can then be pasted on the crown. Help the children make the right size crown by taping or stapling the two end tabs together.

## Discuss/Share

With all the children wearing their crowns, ask what they enjoyed during the lessons on respect and what they learned.

Dance: End with a circle dance while singing "Each One of Us Is Beautiful" or another respect song.

Ending Awareness: When we are experiencing all our wonderful qualities, we feel full of self-respect, and that feels wonderful inside.

Respect

## Sequence of Activities After the Peace and Respect Units

1. **Sing.** Begin or end with a song, as you prefer. Sing songs on the theme of the value with the children, but include the peace, respect and love songs occasionally.

2. **Quietly Being Exercises.** During your values time, alternate daily between the Peace Star exercise and the Respect Star exercise. After the class has done the Love unit, do the Filling Up with Love exercise every third lesson. For your convenience, these are also in the Appendix.

3. **Lesson.** Do one lesson daily, or whatever your schedule permits. Lessons often include a discussion as well as an activity. They are in the recommended order. Feel free to be creative and add your own ideas as well as activities from the culture(s) of the children.

**Circle Time.** Try to provide circle or sharing time once a day—or, if not possible, once a week. It is an excellent beginning for values time. The children can sit in a circle if there are fewer than fifteen, or if more, they can be grouped in front of the teacher. Ask what they feel good about today or what they are proud of. Or ask them to tell how they showed love or peace to someone. Positively acknowledge whatever they share. It is a good time to engage in collaborative rule changes and conflict resolution as needed.

# THREE

# Love Unit

# 3. LOVE UNIT

Reflection Points. . . . . . . . . . . . . . . . . . . . . . . . . . . 62

Objectives . . . . . . . . . . . . . . . . . . . . . . . . . . . . . . 62

**LOVE LESSONS**

Lesson 1    The Happy Sponges. . . . . . . . . . . . . . . . . . 64

Quietly Being    Filling Up with Love Exercise . . . . . . . . . . 65

Lesson 2    I Am Lovable . . . . . . . . . . . . . . . . . . . . . 66

Lesson 3    The Sponge Game. . . . . . . . . . . . . . . . . . 67

Lesson 4    I Feel Full of Love When . . . . . . . . . . . . . 68

Lesson 5    Giving Love . . . . . . . . . . . . . . . . . . . . . 69

Lesson 6    Hearts and Qualities. . . . . . . . . . . . . . . . . 70

Song    True Blue Friend . . . . . . . . . . . . . . . . . . . 71

Lesson 7    Stories . . . . . . . . . . . . . . . . . . . . . . . . 71

Lesson 8    Different Kinds of Hearts . . . . . . . . . . . . . 72

Lesson 9    A Heart Book . . . . . . . . . . . . . . . . . . . . 73

Song    Share . . . . . . . . . . . . . . . . . . . . . . . . . 74

Lesson 10    Love Is Sharing—Heart-Shaped Treats . . . . . 74

Lesson 11    Love Is Caring. . . . . . . . . . . . . . . . . . . . 75

Song    If Someone Says I Love You . . . . . . . . . . . 76

Love

Lesson 12   Conflict Resolution—Thinking with . . . . . . . 76
            Your Heart
Lesson 13   A Flower of Love. . . . . . . . . . . . . . . . . . . 78
Lesson 14   Love Is Caring—Nature . . . . . . . . . . . . . . 79
Lesson 15   I Want What Is Good for You . . . . . . . . . . 80
Lesson 16   Love Is Being Kind . . . . . . . . . . . . . . . . . 81
Lesson 17   Loving Unit Review . . . . . . . . . . . . . . . . . 81

## Love Reflection Points

♦ I am lovable.

♦ I have love inside.

♦ Love is caring.

♦ Love is sharing.

♦ Love is being kind.

♦ Love makes me feel safe.

♦ When there's lots of love inside, anger runs away.

♦ Love means I want what is good for others.

## Love Unit

**GOAL: To increase the experience of love.**

**OBJECTIVES:**

❏ To enjoy the Filling Up with Love exercise, as demonstrated by sitting quietly during the exercise and appearing content in doing so.

❏ To express why they are lovable through words or drawing.

❏ To enjoy the Sponge Game.

Love

**GOAL: To increase knowledge about love.**
**OBJECTIVES:**

❑ To be able to talk about one or more Love Points.

❑ To finish the root sentence, "I feel full of love when _____
_____."

❑ To identify loving things people do during values discussions and activities.

**GOAL: To build sharing and caring social skills.**
**OBJECTIVES:**

❑ To make a heart for parents or caregivers.

❑ To discuss how to do something kind for someone, and to carry out the activity.

❑ To suggest a more appropriate or loving response once the initial negativity in a conflict is identified by others.

# Love Lessons

The Love Reflection Points can be used to help define loving behavior and how it works inside. The points can be used as the first focus point during values time or can be a discussion point as part of language arts. Allow the opportunity to share.

For five- through seven-year-olds, the teacher can choose to use some of the words and sentences as content for reading, spelling and writing.

Love

Lesson

**1**

LOVE LESSON 1

# The Happy Sponges

Say, "The value we will be looking at over the next few weeks is love." Ask:

- Who needs love?
- Who likes to get love?

The responses of the children are likely to be quick, affirmative ones. Acknowledge their responses. Say, "I think we all agree love is important." Tell the children you are going to read them a story.

Read the "The Happy Sponges" story to the children (Appendix).

---

NOTE TO TEACHER

Include a song and a Quietly Being exercise in each lesson as mentioned in "Sequence of Activities."

---

## Discuss/Share

- Where did the sponge live?
- What surprised the sponge when he saw the little girl?
- What did the sponge explain to Marion? When do sponges feel sad?
- What do the sponges do when someone feels sad or angry?
- How were the sponge and Marion the same?

Love

## Activity

Draw or paint pictures about "The Happy Sponges" story.

**Introduce** the Filling Up with Love exercise by saying, "Everyone has love deep inside. But sometimes people forget that it is there, and they don't use it, and so it dries up. And they get sad or angry a lot, because they forgot how to feel all the love that is inside."

- Have you ever become sad? . . . (Wait for their responses and acknowledge.)
- Have you ever become angry? . . .

"Yes, we all get sad and angry sometimes—we forget how we can feel our love inside. So today we're going to practice feeling the love inside. When we feel lots of love inside, it can grow. This inside love is a special love because it makes us love ourselves and our friends and family even more. Ready to practice?"

## Filling Up with Love Exercise

"Everyone sit comfortably and let yourself be still inside. . . . Let's pretend there is a soft rose-colored circle of light all around us. . . . That rose light is full of love. . . . That love is so soft and light and safe. . . . That light reminds the light inside of me that it's full of love, too. . . . I tune into that rose light inside me and enjoy the fullness of the love. . . . I am me. . . . I am naturally full of love. . . . I tune into the beauty inside myself. . . . This rose light of love is always there. . . . Whenever I want to feel more love inside, I can tune into that factory of love inside and make lots more."

The above exercise is also in the Appendix.

Love

NOTE TO TEACHER

## Dealing with a Grumpy Child

If the children are having a grumpy day, you might say: "Do you know what I know when people are grumpy? . . . That there's not enough love inside. Shall we choose love over being grumpy? Okay?. . . But first, does anyone want to share why he or she is grumpy? We're all grumpy sometimes, and that's okay. But we can do something about it, because it isn't much fun. Who would like to share why he or she is grumpy?" . . . (Acknowledge responses, and take care of any real physical needs if there are such. For example, if someone is simply hungry, have snack time first. If someone was fighting, have the children tell how they feel, and resolve the problem using the conflict resolution methods in the Peace unit. Then proceed.) "Let's sit down and go to our inside love factory. I let the cloud of grumpiness start to go away as I picture a soft rose-colored circle of light all around us." . . . (Proceed as above).

Lesson
**2**

LOVE LESSON 2

# I Am Lovable

Discuss the following Love Reflection Point: I am lovable. Ask:

- What does that mean?
- Why are you lovable?

Love

Acknowledge all answers. Add, "And you are all lovable just because you are you." Ask:

- Do you remember your positive qualities from the lessons on Respect?
- Tell me all the positive qualities you can think of. (List them on the board or a big piece of paper.)

Say, "Now I want you to tell me four positive qualities that you have."

## Activity

Draw a picture of yourself, and under it write, "I am lovable because _____

_____." Younger children can tell an adult the sentence they wish to be written.

LOVE LESSON 3

# The Sponge Game

Lesson
3

Begin teaching a song on love. Teach one from your culture.

## Activity

Read "The Happy Sponges" story again.

Love

Then ask the children to make sponges. They can use real sponges or make them out of crumpled colored paper. They can decorate them and add facial features or whatever sparks their imagination.

When the sponges are completed, ask one-third of the children to form a circle with their sponges. They are to stand in a circle. As the other children circle around them, they are to hold their sponges up and feel that their sponge is giving love to each child that passes. Play some happy music or have all the children sing as they do this. Give each one-third of the class a quick turn standing in the middle with their sponges—just two to three minutes. Have a good time.

As this will be a lot of active fun with little children, the teacher might want to do the Peace Star exercise at the end of this activity.

---

## Lesson 4

### LOVE LESSON 4

# I Feel Full of Love When . . .

## Discuss/Share

In a circle group, ask the children to share the things that make them feel loved. Positively affirm their ideas.

**Root Sentence:** Ask the children to stand in a circle and say one sentence beginning with the words, "I feel full of love when

_____

_____."

## Activity

The children could then paint what they talked about. Ask them to stay in the feeling of being full of love while they paint.

LOVE LESSON 5

# Giving Love

Sing a song about love again.

Discuss the meaning of the song: Ask the children to think of examples.

- What are ways we give love?
- What happens when we give someone a smile? (That's right, they smile back.)
- Can you think of a time when you gave love and it came back?
- What happens when we help someone?
- How do you feel when you help?
- Can anyone share a story?
- How do you feel when you need something and someone helps you?

Sing the song again and add hand movements.

Love

LOVE LESSON 6

# Hearts and Qualities

## Discuss/Share

- What kind of world would it be if everyone saw each other's good qualities?

## Activity

Give the children materials to make a paper heart. Allow them to color it, or use colored paper. Play relaxing music as they make their hearts, and help those who need it to write their names on the back.

The teacher should then collect the hearts and put them in a box. Then the teacher takes a heart from the box and gives one to each child. Each child should receive a heart that is different from his or her own. With six- and seven-year-olds, ask them to write a quality of the person whose name is on the heart. If you have a small group of toddlers, discuss the qualities of each child and ask them to draw a picture on the heart before giving it back to the other child. Each child can then place the heart in the form of a big heart on the wall with the teacher's help.

*—Contributed by Dominique Ache and Encarnación Royo Costa*

Love

## Song

### True Blue Friend

Chorus: <sup>C</sup>A true blue friend will <sup>F</sup>always care
And <sup>G</sup>be there for you <sup>C</sup>too.
A <sup>Am</sup>true blue friend is <sup>D</sup>what I think of <sup>G</sup>you,
<sup>F</sup>My <sup>G</sup>friend.

Verse: <sup>F</sup>When I feel <sup>C</sup>sad, <sup>F</sup>you always <sup>C</sup>say,
<sup>F</sup>Let's take a <sup>C</sup>walk <sup>F</sup>or sit and <sup>C</sup>talk,
And <sup>D</sup>then my sadness goes <sup>G</sup>away.
<sup>F</sup>You share <sup>C</sup>cookies, <sup>F</sup>your toys and <sup>C</sup>cake.
You <sup>F</sup>never make <sup>C</sup>fun if I <sup>F</sup>trip when I <sup>C</sup>run,
Or <sup>D</sup>if I make a silly <sup>G</sup>mistake.

---

LOVE LESSON 7

# Stories

Lesson

**7**

Read stories about loving people and loving acts—stories in which love triumphs. Each culture has many stories of that nature. Choose your favorites.

During discussion time, ask the children ways love was shown in the stories. Allow the children to act out the story.

Love

**Lesson 8**

LOVE LESSON 8

# Different Kinds of Hearts

## Discuss/Share

Talk about what it means to be big-hearted, soft-hearted, sad-hearted and mean-hearted. Ask the children what it means to them. Ask:

- How do you feel when you are big-hearted?
- How do you feel when you are sad-hearted?
- What kinds of things do soft-hearted people do?
- What do mean-hearted people need to learn?

> ### NOTE TO TEACHER
>
> If the children are expressing anger or sadness, stop the lesson here and ask them to draw a picture of what they want the mean-hearted people to learn. Continue with the rest of this lesson on the next day.

- What kind of heart do peacemakers have? . . . Yes, you children are big-hearted. Are you soft-hearted, too?
- What kinds of things do big-hearted children do? . . . (They give a smile, hold someone's hand when that person feels bad, get water for someone when that person is thirsty, help Mom . . .)

Love

## Activity

Ask each child to draw or paint a big-hearted heart. They can give it arms and legs and make it do things in their picture or write words around it. Ask them to think of someone they would like to give the picture to. When they give the picture to that person, ask them to tell that person why they think he or she has a big heart.

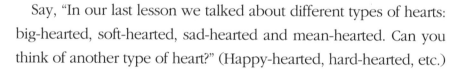

LOVE LESSON 9

# A Heart Book

Lesson
9

## Discuss/Share

Say, "In our last lesson we talked about different types of hearts: big-hearted, soft-hearted, sad-hearted and mean-hearted. Can you think of another type of heart?" (Happy-hearted, hard-hearted, etc.)

## Activity

Instruct four- to seven-year-olds to fold a piece of paper in half twice, thus making a little book. Ask them to draw or paint the four different types of hearts and decide what each one says. An adult could write down the sentence that the child would like under each type of heart. The five- to seven-year-olds might copy that sentence or write their own. With three-year-olds (and the older children if you like), allow each child to make a heart puppet by placing a cut-out heart on a little stick, or make heart figures out of pipe cleaners. The children can play with their heart puppets, giving them different voices depending on which type of heart puppet it is.

Love

## Song

### Share

Chorus:  <sup>Db</sup>It's a beautiful feeling to
Share, share, share
To <sup>Gb</sup>show someone you
<sup>Ab</sup>Care, care, care.
<sup>Db</sup>You can make friends every <sup>Ab</sup>where
When you <sup>Ab</sup>learn to <sup>Db</sup>share.

Verse:  <sup>Ab</sup>Will you share your <sup>Db</sup>toy with me?
<sup>Ab</sup>And I'll share mine with <sup>Db</sup>you.
<sup>Gb</sup>We can <sup>Ab</sup>play <sup>Db</sup>together
<sup>Eb dim</sup>Instead of one toy <sup>Ab</sup>we'll have <sup>Db</sup>two!
<sup>Ab</sup>Isn't that Johnny <sup>Db</sup>walking by?
<sup>Ab</sup>Let's ask him to <sup>Db</sup>play.
<sup>Gb</sup>We'll share <sup>Ab</sup>our toys <sup>Db</sup>with him
And <sup>Eb dim</sup>make a new <sup>Ab</sup>friend <sup>Db</sup>today.
*(Repeat chorus, repeat verse and repeat chorus two times.)*

—*Contributed by Max and Marcia Nass*

---

**Lesson 10**

LOVE LESSON 10

# Love Is Sharing—Heart-Shaped Treats

Discuss the following Love Reflection Point: Love is sharing. Then ask the children to remember a time when someone shared something with them.

- How did you feel?

Love

- What do you like other children to share?
- What do you like your mother (or father or caregiver) to share?
- What do you like to share?
- Is it hard to share sometimes? *(If the reply is "yes," acknowledge the response, "Yes, it is hard to share sometimes. What is easy to share?")*

Today you will all share something, and you will all receive something, too, because we are going to make _____ _____.

## Activity

Create the opportunity for the children to make something to eat which is heart-shaped. You could help them make cookies if there is an oven, or if there is not, they could cut out pieces of bread in heart shapes and spread on a topping. Ask each child to make one for himself or herself and one for someone else. In order to make sure everyone gets one, they could sit in a circle and give one to the person next to them. Or they could visit another class, sharing their heart-shaped treats.

Play the Happy Sponge game.

LOVE LESSON 11

# Love Is Caring

Discuss the following Love Reflection Point: Love is caring.

Love

## Activity

Ask the children to make a heart for their mother or father or caregiver. Use materials available—perhaps they could make one out of clay or could weave one of colored paper or straw.

## Song

### If Someone Says I Love You

DIf someone says, "I love you,
GI want to be your Dfriend,"
GThen my heart is Dhappy,
And Aalso Dcontent.

DLa, la, la, Ala, la,
La la la la Dla la
La, la, Ala, la, la
La Dla la la
DWhen someone says, "You are a lovely star,
GI want to sparkle like Dyou,"
GThen my heart is Dhappy
And Aalso Dcontent.

---

**Lesson 12**

LOVE LESSON 12

# Conflict Resolution—
# Thinking with Your Heart

Do the Filling Up with Love exercise.

Love

Discuss the following Love Reflection Point: When there's love inside, anger runs away. Ask, "Can you think of a time when that happened to you?" Ask the children to share.

## Activity

Say, "Today we will look at how we can use our hearts and our heads together to learn. It's easy to solve conflicts with a little love." Draw a big heart on the floor (large enough for two children to stand in).

Bring up a conflict that occurred (or create a pretend situation). Ask the children involved to think back to the first thing that started the conflict. Do this in a very non-judgmental manner. Praise them for thinking back to identify when the negativity started. Then say, "Now I want you to think of something different that you could do at that very moment the conflict started (first negative statement). When you think of something, step into the heart." Compliment the children when they come up with a loving alternative behavior: "Good thinking with your heart."

---

NOTE TO TEACHER

Continue to use the heart drawn on the floor for any conflicts that occur during the time you are doing this unit.

—*Contributed by Pilar Quera Colomina*

---

Continue the discussion:

- What types of things start a conflict on the playground?
- What types of things start a conflict in the class?

Love

Acknowledge the children's responses. Ask them to think of solutions with their hearts. When they are ready, they can stand in the large heart drawn on the floor and give their solutions.

## Activity

Make symbols for different solutions (hearts, doves). Hold them up. Take turns saying why that is a good solution.

LOVE LESSON 13

# A Flower of Love

## Discuss/Share

- What do you love?
- Who do you love?
- What do you love about yourself?
- How do you take care of something you love?
- How do you speak with people you love?

## Activity

Create flowers, and write or draw on the petals things each child loves.

*—Contributed by Marcia Maria Lins de Medeiros*

Love

LOVE LESSON 14

# Love Is Caring—Nature

## Discuss/Share

- What do you love about nature?
- How do we care for nature?

---

### NOTE TO TEACHER

Most of the nature activities are in the Simplicity unit.

---

## Activity

If there are trees nearby in a park or forest, perhaps the class can visit, taking a walk in silence or lying down under the trees to observe what they love about nature. If you ask the children to be silent, make it a short time.

Create an opportunity for the children to care for nature, perhaps using one of their ideas during the discussion. Perhaps they would like to commit to not littering, or perhaps the class would like to plant and care for a few flowers. Or they could be careful to step around new plants, or . . . ?

Love

LOVE LESSON 15

# I Want What Is Good for You

Discuss the following Love Reflection Point: Love means I want what is good for others.

- What does that mean?
- Think of someone that's loving. What is he or she like? What kind of things does that person do?
- What do you want for the person you love?

Acknowledge their responses and expand on this theme.

- Does your mother (father, caregiver) want you to eat things that are good for you? Why? (That's right. He or she loves you and wants you to be healthy. He or she wants what is good for you.)
- Does your father (mother, caregiver) want you to smoke? Why not?

## Activity

Ask the children to role-play as the person who wants something good for them. They can enact various roles: mother and child, father and child, child and child, etc.

## LOVE LESSON 16
# Love Is Being Kind

Discuss the following Love Reflection Point: Love is being kind. Ask the children to think of ways to show love. Perhaps helping to get things for our moms and dads when they are ill; being helpful and doing extra chores when someone is busy; saying hello to our guests; being friendly to a new child in school; making a card for someone who is ill, a child who is moving, or . . . ?

## Activity

Create ideas pertinent to your situation and the ages of the children, and carry out one of those ideas.

After the discussion, sing a song.

## LOVE LESSON 17
# Loving Unit Review

## Discuss/Share

- What did you enjoy most during our time on Love in the last few weeks?
- What did you learn?
- What kind of world would it be if everyone had love for each other?

Love

## Activities

Name each child and positively affirm the things he or she did.

Sing a song on love and dance to it.

Play the Sponge Game or another activity the children enjoyed.

End with the Filling Up with Love exercise.

# FOUR

# Responsibility Unit

# 4. RESPONSIBILITY UNIT

Reflection Points. . . . . . . . . . . . . . . . . . . . . . . . . . . 86

Objectives . . . . . . . . . . . . . . . . . . . . . . . . . . . . . . . 86

**RESPONSIBILITY LESSONS**

Lesson 1   I Feel Proud When . . . . . . . . . . . . . . . . . . 88

Lesson 2   The Seeing Eyes . . . . . . . . . . . . . . . . . . . 89

Lesson 3   Advice to Dog Owners of the World . . . . . . 90

Lesson 4   A Better World . . . . . . . . . . . . . . . . . . . 91

Lesson 5   Caring for the Home Corner . . . . . . . . . . . 92

Lesson 6   Trying My Best . . . . . . . . . . . . . . . . . . . 93

Lesson 7   Good, Responsible Helpers. . . . . . . . . . . . 94

Lesson 8   Thinking About Responsibilities . . . . . . . . 95

Lesson 9   Appreciating My Parent's Responsibility . . . . 96

Lesson 10  My Responsibilities at Home. . . . . . . . . . . 97

Lesson 11  Responsible Choices . . . . . . . . . . . . . . . . 97

Lesson 12  Helping Others . . . . . . . . . . . . . . . . . . . 98

Responsibility

## Responsibility Reflection Points

♦ Responsibility is doing my job.

♦ Responsibility is caring.

♦ Responsibility is trying my best.

♦ Responsibility is doing my share of the work.

♦ Responsibility is taking care of things.

♦ Responsibility is helping others when they need help.

♦ Responsibility is being fair.

♦ Responsibility is helping to make a better world.

## Responsibility Unit

### GOAL: To increase the experience of responsibility.
### OBJECTIVES:

❏ To state what they feel proud of doing.

❏ To feel they are caring when doing the guide-dog activity or another one of the activities.

❏ To experience satisfaction helping somebody with something.

### GOAL: To increase knowledge about responsibility.
### OBJECTIVES:

❏ To identify one responsibility of a student at school and at home.

❏ To identify one responsibility of a teacher.

❏ To be able to talk about one or two Responsibility Points.

❏ To be able to identify the main responsibility of a firefighter and a nurse.

❏ To identify one way the child helps to make a better world.

❑ To make a card for a parent about something the parent does which the child appreciates.

**GOAL: To build responsibility.**

**OBJECTIVES:**

❑ To do an exercise cleaning and caring for materials they use.

❑ To put back the toys they use when asked individually or in a group.

❑ To say something positive to the self when a task is experienced as hard.

❑ For children who usually make little effort, to increase effort and persistence by at least twenty percent.

# Responsibility Lessons

Responsibility Reflection Points can be used to help define that value. The points can be used as the first focus point during values time or can be a discussion point as part of language arts. Allow the opportunity to share.

For five- through seven-year-olds, the teacher can choose to use some of the words and sentences as content for reading, spelling and writing. As the students continue with the unit, they can create their own Responsibility Reflection Points. They can then draw or write those or make up short stories.

Responsibility

# I Feel Proud When . . .

## Discuss/Share

- What is responsibility?
- What does that mean?

Use the Reflection Reflection Points to help define this word. For example, "Responsibility is doing my job. Each one of us has different jobs in life."

Ask the following questions, acknowledging their answers.

- As the teacher, what is my job? What am I responsible for? ("That's right. I come to school to teach you. And I teach you your numbers and letters, and _____. Yes, and I _____.")
- Can you think of other things teachers are responsible for? ("Yes, helping children, giving grades, _____.")
- And you are the students. What are you responsible for? What is your job as a student?
- Very good. Who can think of another responsibility?
- How do you feel when you do a good job?

Say, "It's a good feeling to feel happy and proud of yourself. Each one of you is capable, lovable and knows how to be responsible."

**Root Sentence:** Ask the children to think about a time when they were proud of helping, that is, proud of being responsible.

Responsibility

Ask them to stand in a circle. Ask each child in the circle to take a turn saying the root sentence, "I feel proud when I _____ _____."

End with a song on love or respect.

---

NOTE TO TEACHER

Include a song and a Quietly Being exercise in each lesson.

---

RESPONSIBILITY LESSON 2

# The Seeing Eyes

Lesson 2

Discuss the following Responsibility Reflection Points:

♦ Responsibility is doing my job.
♦ Responsibility is caring.

## Activity

**Explain** to the children how a Seeing Eye dog (a guide dog) helps a blind person. The dog is very responsible and acts in a caring way for the blind person. He guides him or her down a safe path and stops at the streets and the stairs. He does not run after rabbits or other dogs when it is time to help the blind person. The dog only runs and plays when it is time to play. To practice being responsible and to know how important that is, let's play Seeing Eyes.

Ask each child to pair up with another child. One pretends to be the Seeing Eye dog, and the other pretends to be the blind

Responsibility

person. (Older children may use blindfolds. With very young children, do not use a blindfold, but tell them to close their eyes and pretend to be a blind person. In this way, they can open their eyes if they do not feel safe.) The "blind" child can put his or her hand on the shoulder of the "pretend dog." Then they change roles. Ask:

- How did you feel as the "pretend guide dog?"
- How did you feel as the blind person when the "pretend guide dog" was careful and responsible?
- Was anyone afraid the "pretend guide dog" would not be responsible?
- What kinds of things do you want your guide dog to do?

Acknowledge, "Yes, we feel safer when people around us are responsible."

---

## Lesson 3

### RESPONSIBILITY LESSON 3
# Advice to Dog Owners of the World

Discussion: "In the last lesson, you took turns being the pretend guide dogs." Ask:

- If you were a guide dog, how would you want your owner to treat you?
- What things would a responsible pet owner make sure to do? (Feed the dog. Make sure it has water. Make sure the harness is not too tight.)

Responsibility

- If you were to tell all the dog owners of the world what dogs needed, what would you tell them? (Make sure petting them is included!)

## Activity

Draw a picture of a dog and all the ways it would like its owner to be responsible. Older children can write under it: Be responsible. The teacher of younger children may want to make a sheet for the children to cut out and/or color, including a dog and various items such as a food bowl, a heart, etc.

RESPONSIBILITY LESSON 4

# A Better World

Lesson

4

Discuss the following Responsibility Reflection Point: Responsibility is helping to make a better world.

- What does that mean?
- What can we do to make a better world?

Acknowledge their replies. Say, "I want you to think of a person that you like very much. What is it about that person that you like? . . . (Acknowledge their replies.) Yes, it can be their smile, or the love they give, or _____. You all have wonderful smiles. Each smile makes it a better world, doesn't it?"

- Part of our world is our class (or our school). What can we do to make a better class (school)?

Acknowledge their ideas.

*Responsibility*

## Activity

Think about which project(s) you would like implemented in the class. A project that reinforces the above idea is planting a few flowers. The children could take responsibility for planting and watering the flowers.

### RESPONSIBILITY LESSON 5

# Caring for the Home Corner

Discuss the following Responsibility Reflection Point: Responsibility is taking care of things.

**Awareness:** I have the right to play with and enjoy all the toys, but I also have the responsibility to keep everything tidy, clean and in good condition. We can help each other to make things and keep them in good condition.

## Activity

Ask the children to clean and care for the materials they use. For example, in nursery school, small groups of children with a teacher could wash the plastic dolls and doll clothes in a bowl and hang them out to dry. Others could wash the toy cooking utensils. Others could clean the playhouse. Children ages six and seven could mend the books, clean the paint or toy area, etc.

At circle time, the children can share why they like the things they cared for, why those things are important to them and what makes them break. They may choose to decide how to use and respect things.

RESPONSIBILITY LESSON 6

# Trying My Best

## Discuss/Share

- What are your responsibilities at school?
- How do you feel when you do a good job?
- What do you say to yourself then?
- How do you feel when something is hard?
- What do you say to yourself then?
- What positive things can you say to yourself when something is hard?

Add a couple of your own thoughts, or ask the children to repeat the following sentences.

- I can learn this.
- This is hard right now. But because I try, it will get easy.
- I can do it.

**Explain:** "Sometimes people stop being responsible because they think something is hard and they can't do it. But everyone has things that are hard for them to do. When you were much smaller you could not do the things you can do now. As you get bigger, you will be able to do even more things. One of the Responsibility Points is: Responsibility is trying my best. I'm going to tell you a story about someone who knew how to try."

Responsibility

Story: Read "The Little Engine that Could," "The Tortoise and the Hare," or another story from your culture about someone who kept trying.

Discuss the story, and then ask:

- Did anyone think of something else positive you could say to yourself when something is hard?
- Anyone else?

Acknowledge their responses and list them on a board.

## Activity

Ask the children to draw a picture about the story, or the teacher can draw a picture for the children to color and cut out. Or ask the children to act out the story.

---

Lesson

7

RESPONSIBILITY LESSON 7

# Good, Responsible Helpers

Review the children's favorite positive sayings from the prior lesson. Write them on a poster.

Discuss the following Responsibility Reflection Point: Responsibility is doing my share of the work.

Ask the children to help you think of all the things they can help with in the classroom. Think of age-appropriate tasks, such as getting the materials, passing around materials, stirring things, wiping the tables and putting away toys. The children can help identify other tasks, and responsibility for carrying them out can be rotated among the children.

A light attitude on the part of the adults and positive affirmation of the children as "good, responsible helpers" builds a cadre of enthusiastic, willing workers.

Give children the responsibility of taking out their toys and putting them away. For very small children, you can start with one toy taken from one place. Initially it will be necessary to prompt them to take it down and put it back. As they develop the routine, offer a choice of two toys or games. Praise or positively notice their tidying efforts.

RESPONSIBILITY LESSON 8

# Thinking About Responsibilities

Discuss the following Responsibility Reflection Point: Responsibility is doing my job. Talk about how people in a school or a daycare center share the work. Ask:

- What is the responsibility of the teacher?
- What is the responsibility of Mr. (or Ms.) _____?
- What is the responsibility of a firefighter?
- What is the responsibility of a doctor?

## Activity

Select various professions that you think children of that age would know about in their community, such as firefighters, nurses, etc. Select elements of their uniforms for the children to make, such as a firefighter's hat. Or improvise uniforms from your "dress up" area if there is one in the classroom. Or ask the

*Responsibility*

children to make pictures of a profession and share with the rest of the class, "If I were a firefighter, look what I would do . . ." "If I were a nurse, my responsibility would be to _____ _____."

*—Contributed by Encarnación Royo Costa*

RESPONSIBILITY LESSON 9

# Appreciating My Parent's Responsibility

## Discuss/Share

State, "In families, the members of the family share the work, too. Sometimes that means going to work to earn money to pay for the house and food, and sometimes that means cooking and cleaning, fixing things and taking care of the children."

- How are mothers responsible?
- What kinds of things do they do?
- How are fathers responsible?
- What kinds of things do they do?
- Who else is responsible for things in your family?
- What do they do?

## Activity

Ask the children to make a card for a parent or other family member. Perhaps they can make a picture of their parent doing something the child appreciates.

*Responsibility*

## RESPONSIBILITY LESSON 10

# My Responsibilities at Home

### Discuss/Share

Children are responsible at home, too. Ask:

- What is your responsibility at home?
- Is your chore putting away your toys?
- Are you old enough to make your bed?
- How else do you help?

### Activity

Create the opportunity to have the children make cutouts of the activities they described. These can begin to make a mural, entitled "We Are Responsible."

## RESPONSIBILITY LESSON 11

# Responsible Choices

Discuss the following Responsibility Reflection Point: Responsibility is being fair. Then talk about the rules in the classroom and discuss them.

- Which rules are fair?
- Which ones do you like? Why?
- What are the good things that happen because we have the rules?

*Responsibility*

- What things might happen if there was the rule _____?
- Are there other rules you would like?
- Are there other things you think we should do? (And if so, what are they?)
- How do you think we could do that?
- Would that solution work? Why? Why not?

*—Contributed by Dominique Ache*

Follow up on your discussion and decisions the next week at circle time. How is it working?

---

**Lesson 12**

RESPONSIBILITY LESSON 12

# Helping Others

Discuss the Responsibility Reflection Points:

♦ Responsibility is being caring.
♦ Responsibility is helping others when they need help.

## Activity

Develop a sense of responsibility in the older children by allowing them to help the younger ones. In a daycare center, four-year-olds can be very helpful with three-year-olds. Create an opportunity for the children to help others.

# FIVE

# Happiness Unit

# 5. HAPPINESS UNIT

Reflection Points. . . . . . . . . . . . . . . . . . . . . . . . . 102
Objectives . . . . . . . . . . . . . . . . . . . . . . . . . . . 102

**HAPPINESS LESSONS**

Lesson 1   Act It Out . . . . . . . . . . . . . . . . . . . . 104
Song       Happy Children. . . . . . . . . . . . . . . . 105
Lesson 2   Using Our Imagination . . . . . . . . . . . 105
Lesson 3   Happiness Is Knowing . . . . . . . . . . . 106
Lesson 4   Happy Games . . . . . . . . . . . . . . . . . 107
Song       Smile . . . . . . . . . . . . . . . . . . . . . . 108
Lesson 5   Words Can Be Like Flowers or Thorns . . . . 109
Lesson 6   The Heart School. . . . . . . . . . . . . . . 110
Lesson 7   The Golden Bear . . . . . . . . . . . . . . . 111
Song       The Rainbow Song. . . . . . . . . . . . . . 111
Lesson 8   Happy Boxes. . . . . . . . . . . . . . . . . . 112
Lesson 9   Cards for the Happy Boxes . . . . . . . . . . 113
Lesson 10  Story. . . . . . . . . . . . . . . . . . . . . . . 115
Lesson 11  Sharing. . . . . . . . . . . . . . . . . . . . . . 115
Lesson 12  Good Wishes. . . . . . . . . . . . . . . . . . 116

Happiness

Song        The Happy Stars . . . . . . . . . . . . . . . . . 117

Lesson 13   Stories. . . . . . . . . . . . . . . . . . . . . . 118

Lesson 14   Heart School Drawings. . . . . . . . . . . . . 118

Lesson 15   Happy Star Dance . . . . . . . . . . . . . . . 119

## Happiness Reflection Points

♦ When I have love and peace inside, happiness just comes.

♦ Happiness is having fun with my friends.

♦ Happiness is knowing I am loved.

♦ When I do good things, I am happy with myself.

♦ Good wishes for everyone make me happy inside.

♦ I can give happiness to everyone with my good wishes.

♦ I can give happiness to others with words that are like flowers, not thorns.

♦ I can give happiness to others by sharing.

## Happiness Unit

**GOAL: To enjoy the experience of happiness.**

**OBJECTIVES:**

❏ To enjoy the Imagining a Happy World exercise.

❏ To enjoy games with the children in the class.

❏ To sing two songs that generate a happy feeling.

**GOAL: To increase knowledge about happiness.**

**OBJECTIVES:**

❏ To be able to communicate in words or through drawing what a happy world would look and feel like.

❏ To identify several good things he or she does as part of

participating in a discussion on the Happiness Reflection Point: When I do good things, I am happy with myself.

❏ To explore our feelings when people say mean things or nice things.

❏ To generate at least three ideas about how we can give happiness.

**GOAL: To build social skills for happy relationships.**
**OBJECTIVES:**

❏ To identify words or phases which hurt others, and other words or phrases which give happiness.

❏ To participate in class discussions on how we can be patient with ourselves and with others.

❏ To practice having good wishes for everyone in the class during Quietly Being exercises.

❏ To be able to use an assertive phrase, such as "Give me flowers, not thorns," if a classmate says something unkind.

# Happiness Lessons

Happiness Reflection Points can be used in talking about what makes us happy and how we can give happiness. The points can be used as the first focus point during values time or can be a discussion point as part of language arts. Allow the opportunity to share.

For five- through seven-year-olds, the teacher can choose to use some of the words and sentences as content for reading, spelling and writing. As the students continue with the unit, they can create their own Happiness Reflection Points. They can then draw or write those or make up short stories.

HAPPINESS LESSON 1

# Act It Out

Begin with the Filling Up with Love exercise.

**Explain:** "In the next four weeks (or whatever length of time), we're going to learn more about happiness. Our first Happiness Reflection Point is":

- When I have love and peace inside, happiness just comes.

## Discuss/Share

- What does that mean?
- Can anyone tell me about that?
- Can you think of a time that happened?

## Activity

In a circle group, ask the children to share the things that make them happy. Ask each child to act it out from his or her chair or in the middle of the circle. Their responses might include a smile, a hug or a fun game. Acknowledge their responses. Lead the applause.

In a circle group, ask the children to share how they give happiness. Ask them to act it out with the child sitting next to them.

Sing a song on happiness from your culture, or you might want to sing the following.

### Happy Children

ᴰDo you see the happy children,
ᴬ⁷Getting up to dance around,
ᴰAll they want is to be happy,
And to ᴬ⁷swing and swing around.

ᴳBend right down and ᴰtouch your toes,
ᴬ⁷Touch your knees and ᴰtouch your nose,
ᴳClap your hands and ᴰshake them out,
ᴱ⁷Stand upright and ᴬ⁷turn around . . .
*(Repeat)*

---

NOTE TO TEACHER

Include a song during each lesson and do a Quietly Being exercise every day.

---

HAPPINESS LESSON 2

# Using Our Imagination

Ask the children to sit comfortably or lie on the floor.

"Today we're going to use our imagination again to make a picture in our mind. Let yourself get comfortable and let the body be very still. . . . Imagine a big, beautiful butterfly. It can be any color you like. This butterfly likes to fly to places where only happy people live. Do you want to go there, too? . . . Okay, close your eyes and listen. Imagine you are sitting on the wings of this big, beautiful, colorful butterfly and are flying to a place where children are happy. . . . Now you have arrived. . . . Can

*Happiness*

you see the happy faces of the children? . . . Now the butterfly comes to rest on the grass in this beautiful world, and all the children come to welcome the butterfly and to welcome you. . . . What do they say to you? . . . The children ask you to play with them. . . . What are you playing? . . . Now they call you to join a picnic on the grass. . . . What do you eat? . . . What do you say to each other? . . . Now you look around. . . . You see trees, flowers . . . birds . . . the sun. . . . Is your face looking happy? . . . Now it's time to come back to school (or camp or wherever the setting is). You sit on the wings of your loving butterfly, and off you fly back here. Now open your eyes, and we will share."

## Discuss/Share

Ask the children to share their experiences.

## Activity

Provide the opportunity for children to make butterflies or a picture of a happy world. Paper wings of a butterfly can be painted or colored and attached to an ice cream stick. The butterflies can be used as a Quietly Being symbol, or used to role-play conversations.

Lesson
3

HAPPINESS LESSON 3

# Happiness Is Knowing

## Discuss/Share

Say, "When we did the unit on respect, we learned that part of respect is knowing we are lovable and capable. Each one of us is loved. But let's talk about who loves you. One of the

Happiness Reflection Points is: Happiness is knowing I am loved."

- What does that mean?
- Why do you think that's true?
- Who loves you?
- Does everyone need to be loved?

## Activity

Ask the children to draw a picture of themselves with someone who loves them.

**Homework:** Tell the children that their homework for today is to give someone at home one extra hug.

**Hug Homework:** When they come back the next day, ask the children to tell what happened with their hug homework. Ask, "Is giving a hug to someone we love one of the ways we can give happiness?" If you get a resounding yes, tell the children that their homework for today again is to give someone at home one extra hug. When they come back the next day, ask them what happened, and give them the same homework every day for that week.

HAPPINESS LESSON 4

# Happy Games

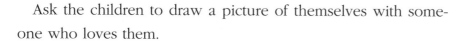

Discuss the following Happiness Reflection Point: Happiness is having fun with my friends.

Happiness

## Activity

Play a game that everyone loves, which brings lots of laughter. You know the ones they love. Many children enjoy Duck, Duck, Goose. In this game, all the children sit in a circle. One child walks around the outside of the circle and gently taps the other children on the top of the head. Each time the child taps, he or she says duck or goose. The child may say duck one or ten times, but as soon as he or she says goose, the child tapped gets up to chase the tapping child around the circle. The tapping child tries to run all the way around the circle to sit in the place of the child who was called goose. The tapping child may stay there if he or she reaches there without being tagged. Then the other child continues the game by tapping children and saying, duck, duck, duck . . . goose. If tagged, the child must take a turn tapping again.

An adaptation of the game Hide-and-Seek is fun. One person hides and all the rest look for him or her. When the hiding person is found by one child, instead of that ending the game, that person also hides with the hiding person. The game is over when all the children are hiding together. With small groups of little children, the end of the game is a perfect time for forming a circle, holding hands and singing a song.

## Song

### Smile

Chorus:    ^AThe world needs your ^Esmile
           To ^Dbremind ^Aeveryone
           That we're ^Dbhere to be ^Ahappy

Happiness

So ^E7^smile and have ^A^fun

The ^A^world needs your ^E^smile

^Db^Smile all day ^A^through

^Db^And watch the ^A^whole world

E7Smile back at ^A^you.

Verse:    ^Db^Smile, ^A^smile, ^Db^smile at ^A^everyone

^Db^Smile, ^A^smile, ^Db^smile and have ^A^fun

^Db^Smile, ^A^smile, ^Db^smile all day ^A^through

^Db^Smile, ^A^smile, ^Db^the world smiles at ^A^you.

*(Repeat chorus, repeat verse, repeat chorus two times.)*

—*Contributed by Max and Marcia Nass*

---

HAPPINESS LESSON 5

# Words Can Be Like Flowers or Thorns

Lesson

**5**

Introduce the topic, "Part of happiness comes with words. You were telling me the other day that . . . (Give some examples of what they shared in the circle group: that they feel happy when their mother says she loves them, when their uncle says they're special, etc.) . . . I notice that Jamie likes it when Mario says . . . (Give more specific examples.) So words can give happiness. It's almost like giving a flower . . . or sometimes words can hurt, like a thorn."

## Ask

- What kinds of words make you feel bad or sad?
- What kinds of words make you angry?

*Happiness*

- What kinds of words can you say to others that give happiness?

Say, "Those are some nice things to say. One of the Happiness Reflection Points is:"

- I can give happiness to others with words that are like flowers, not thorns.
- Would anyone like to share about that?

"This week, I'd like us all to pay special attention to giving flowers. If someone does say something mean, you can just say, 'Give me flowers, not thorns.'" The adult can reinforce this, encouraging children to use this as a verbal skill, rather than hitting or saying something mean when others say something negative. Ask the children to repeat the phrase several times.

## Activity

Ask the children to draw a picture about the lesson today. (Some children may draw a time when they felt bad, while others may draw about feeling happy. Allow them to draw whatever they wish.)

Lesson 6

HAPPINESS LESSON 6

# The Heart School

**Review:** Talk about the phrase the children learned in the prior lesson. Ask them to repeat several times the phrase, "Give me flowers, not thorns."

Happiness

Read the first part of "The Heart School" story to the children (Appendix).

Discuss the part of the story read.

## Activity

Make a little Golden Bear out of card paper with movable arms and legs. Paper clips can be used to fix arms and legs to the body.

---

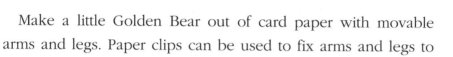

HAPPINESS LESSON 7

# The Golden Bear

Finish reading "The Heart School" story to the children.

## Discuss/Share

- What would the Golden Bear say to you?
- What does patience mean?
- How can we be patient with ourselves?
- How do we feel when others are not patient with us?
- How can we be patient with others?

Begin learning "The Rainbow Song."

### The Rainbow Song

ᴬA smile is like a rainbow
And thoughts like butterflies
And kind words are like flowers

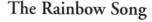

When I am golden and <sup>E</sup>light!
So <sup>A</sup>let's slide up the rainbow
And let us butterfly
And shower all with flowers
Let's be golden and <sup>E</sup>light!
Golden and <sup>D</sup>light
<sup>E</sup>Golden and <sup>A</sup>light
If you sing this song
You'll be like me
Nice to be so happy and free
Sing this song and be like me
<sup>E</sup>Golden and <sup>A</sup>light!

---

Lesson

**8**

HAPPINESS LESSON 8

# Happy Boxes

Begin with "The Rainbow Song."

## Discuss/Share

Talk about the story, and talk about all the things that Marc did that helped him be happier. Then ask the children if they can think of things that would make them happier in class. Write all the suggestions down on a large sheet of paper and discuss them.

**Planning Actions:** Talk about all the suggestions from the former lesson's discussion. Cross out the suggestions that are not practical and focus your attention on the practical ones. Choosing one at a time, think of and share your ideas about them, and then make a plan of how to put your ideas into action. Success is easily achieved if the whole class or group works on the same plan. That creates enthusiasm and a sense of unity.

## Activity

The teacher can decide whether he or she wants the children to make individual Happy and Unhappy Boxes or one Happy Box and one Unhappy Box for the class. Decorate them as you wish. Help the children write their ideas for happiness on little slips of paper that go into the Happy Box. Begin making the boxes.

HAPPINESS LESSON 9

# Cards for the Happy Boxes

Lesson
9

## Activity

Finish making the Happy and Unhappy Boxes and decorate them.

## Discuss/Share

In "The Heart School Story," Marc learns that it is important not to get upset with himself or anyone else. Ask:

- What did Marc learn to do? (To sit together, reflect briefly on what went wrong, and then focus attention on progress and not on mistakes made.)
- Shall we do that, too?

Happiness

## Activity

Ask the children to write cards for the Happy Box, putting a practical suggestion that would make them happier on each card. Help them as needed. You may want to put one-word suggestions for the youngest children, perhaps adding a little picture. Put them into the Happy Box.

Arrange for each child to select one card from the Happy Box, if it is a Happy Box for the whole class, or one child from each group if there are several boxes. Share ideas within your group or class, and make an action plan together in order to achieve what is written on the card.

End with "The Rainbow Song."

---

NOTE TO TEACHER

Many classes will have a discussion time during their values time at this point. You may wish to keep the Happy and Unhappy Boxes for your class if the children like them and appear to benefit. Either daily or weekly, take one card out of the box. Try this for at least four weeks. At least once a week share your experiences and progress with each other, and also look for areas that need improvement. As the children discover new ways to be happy, ask them to write those down on new cards.

---

HAPPINESS LESSON 10

# Story

Read the story, "Billy the Bully," in the Appendix. It is suitable for five-, six- and seven-year-olds.

Discuss the following Happiness Reflection Point in relation to the story: When I do good things, I am happy with myself. Ask:

- What good things do you do that make you happy with yourself?
- What good things do you do at school?
- What good things do you do at home?
- What good things do you do for the world?

List the things the children say on the board.

## Activity

Instruct the children to draw a picture about the good things they do.

HAPPINESS LESSON 11

# Sharing

**Introduction:** Say, "Today we're going to talk about sharing. Every day we share things at school—we share our smiles, and we share tables and crayons and scissors." Ask:

- What else do we share?
- When do you like to share?
- Is it hard to share sometimes? When? (Affirm their responses, such as, "Yes, sometimes it's hard to share our very favorite thing.")
- When is it easy to share?

Discuss the following Happiness Reflection Point: I can give happiness to others by sharing.

Then ask the children what they would like to share. Perhaps they would like to practice sharing during playtime, think about another way to share the toys, bring something to share from home or make something in class they can share such as sweets or cards.

Keep in mind that many children are not ready to share developmentally until they are four or five years old. The teacher can make the sharing easy by having enough of the same things (such as cookies).

HAPPINESS LESSON 12

# Good Wishes

Say, "A secret that hardly anyone knows is that it's easy to be happy if you have good wishes for everyone."

Discuss two Happiness Reflection Points:

♦ Good wishes for everyone make me happy inside.
♦ I can give happiness to everyone with my good wishes.

Happiness

- What does that mean?
- Can anyone tell us about a time when everyone had good wishes for you?
- What did that feel like?
- How do we give happiness to others with our good wishes?

"So, let's fill ourselves up with love like we did last week." Do the Filling Up with Love exercise.

Say, "Now I want you to look around the room at everyone, and just think of them with love. . . . (Allow time for everyone to do that.) Isn't that easy? How does that feel? . . . Okay, let's end with a happy song."

Sing this song or another song on happiness from your culture.

## The Happy Stars

$^G$I am happy, I am happy,
I am a $^{D7}$star,
I am happy, I am happy,
I am a star.
I am happy to remember
to $^C$sparkle forever,
I am $^G$happy, I am $^{D7}$happy,
I am a $^G$star.
I give my love to $^G$everyone,
I give it $^{D7}$from my heart.
I $^G$give my sparkle to everyone,
and $^{D7}$make them sparkle too.
*(Repeat first verse)*

Happiness

## Activity

Allow the children to use finger paints to make a picture of happiness.

HAPPINESS LESSON 13

# Stories

Tell your favorite happy story from when you were a child. Use stories from different cultures.

HAPPINESS LESSON 14

# Heart School Drawings

Begin with "The Rainbow Song."
Pick out a card from the Happy Box and discuss it.

## Activity

A whole group of children (not more than six) can draw the Heart School and its surroundings together on a large piece of paper or card. Or draw any other situation from the story the group liked.

HAPPINESS LESSON 15

# Happy Star Dance

## Discuss/Share

Allow each child to share his or her finger painting. Place them on the wall in the form of a star.

Sing the Happy Star song again.

**Dance:** Once the children know the above song and can sing it from memory, they can dance to it as well. **Actions:** Children skip around in a circle facing inward and turn outward when singing the first "star." The children then skip in the opposite direction. They crouch down when singing the second "star," then rise slowly, bringing their arms up over their heads. They hold both hands again and continue to skip around, stopping on "star" and turning to face inward again.

**For the second verse:** The girls can hold their skirts out, and the children sway from side to side. They then turn around facing outward, and slowly raise their arms toward the ceiling, twiddling their fingers at the same time. Children turn around to face inward again.

Happiness

# SIX

# Cooperation Unit

# 6. COOPERATION UNIT

Reflection Points. . . . . . . . . . . . . . . . . . . . . . . . . . 124
Objectives . . . . . . . . . . . . . . . . . . . . . . . . . . . . . 124

**COOPERATION LESSONS**

Lesson 1    Cooperative Eating. . . . . . . . . . . . . . . . . 126

Song    Star Song . . . . . . . . . . . . . . . . . . . . . 127

Lesson 2    Water to the Horse. . . . . . . . . . . . . . . . . 128

Lesson 3    Stories. . . . . . . . . . . . . . . . . . . . . . . 129

Lesson 4    Cooperative Building . . . . . . . . . . . . . . 129

Lesson 5    Cooking Together . . . . . . . . . . . . . . . 130

Lesson 6    Painting a Butterfly . . . . . . . . . . . . . 130

Lesson 7    Cooperative Games . . . . . . . . . . . . . . . 131

Lesson 8    More Cooperative Games . . . . . . . . . . . 131

Lesson 9    Can I Help You? . . . . . . . . . . . . . . . 133

Lesson 10    Puzzles. . . . . . . . . . . . . . . . . . . . . . 134

Lesson 11    Puzzles Continue . . . . . . . . . . . . . . . 135

Lesson 12    Cooperation at Home. . . . . . . . . . . . . . 135

Lesson 13    Cooperative Mural . . . . . . . . . . . . . . 136

Lesson 14    Cooperative Mural Continues . . . . . . . . . 137

Cooperation

Lesson 15    Cooperation Builders . . . . . . . . . . . . . . . 137

Lesson 16    Cooperative World Race . . . . . . . . . . . . 137

Lesson 17    Cooperation Review . . . . . . . . . . . . . . . 138

## Cooperation Reflection Points

♦ Cooperation is everyone helping to get something done.

♦ Cooperation is working together toward a common goal.

♦ Cooperation is working together with patience and affection.

## Cooperation Unit

### GOAL: To experience cooperation.
### OBJECTIVES:

❑ To have a good time cooperating while playing the cooperation games.

❑ To work cooperatively with several children while making a large butterfly.

❑ To enjoy cooperative eating during the game of unbending elbows.

### GOAL: To increase knowledge about cooperation.
### OBJECTIVES:

❑ To understand that cooperation is sometimes necessary—for example, when a heavy table needs to be moved.

❑ To figure out how to move cooperatively when one of your ankles is tied to someone else's, as measured by being able to stay upright while moving to keep a ball in motion.

❑ To identify words or phrases that make us feel good when working and playing together.

Cooperation

**GOAL: To build social cooperation skills.**

**OBJECTIVES:**

❏ To be pleasant and demonstrate positive cooperative social skills while taking a turn at the Cooperation Table.

❏ To use a polite tone of voice and language when asking for help at the Cooperation Table.

❏ To share materials while working with others in building a house of blocks or other cooperative building activities.

❏ To accept positive comments and make at least two positive comments.

❏ To cooperatively respond to the teacher when asked to help clean something up, as measured by doing so gladly and starting to do so within the specified time.

# Cooperation Lessons

Cooperation Reflection Points can be used to help define that value. The points can be used as the first focus point during values time or can be a discussion point as part of language arts. Allow the opportunity to share.

For five- through seven-year-olds, the teacher can choose to use some of the words and sentences as content for reading, spelling and writing. As the students continue with the unit, they can create their own Cooperation Reflection Points. They can then draw or write those or make up short stories.

## COOPERATION LESSON 1
# Cooperative Eating

**Explain:** "In the next four weeks (or whatever length of time), we're going to learn about cooperation. Cooperation means everyone helping to get something done. Cooperation is very important because we can't do everything alone."

**Demonstrate:** The teacher can illustrate with something in the room that would be too heavy to lift for one child. "Suppose David is in charge of selling things for a fair, and he wants this big table over there instead of here. Does he need cooperation? . . . How many would like to cooperate? . . . Very good. Okay, let's see the difference. With one person, moving the table is very hard—with ten it will be easy." Ask ten children to gather around the table, slip their hands under it and lift it.

Say, "We all need cooperation sometimes." Ask, "When do you need cooperation?" (They might mention homework, putting a kite together, lacing up boots, building a tree house.)

Say, "Today we're going to have a snack (or lunch) that shows how important cooperation is. I want you to pretend that your elbows do not work. They cannot bend. You have to figure out how you're going to eat without bending your elbows! How are you going to do that?"

## Activity

Give them the snack and let them figure it out. If they do not after five or six minutes, model for them keeping your arms straight and getting fed by someone else while you feed the other person. This activity should provide a lot of laughter while learning!

Ask, "Is it more fun if the person who helps is happy to help or grumpy or mad?"

Say, "Real cooperation is working together with patience and affection—happily."

**Sing:** Introduce this song with the idea that cooperation with patience and affection is something that makes us shine.

### Star Song

We are the $^D$stars that shine so $^{A7}$brightly,

We are the stars up in the $^D$sky,

We are the $^{D7}$stars that shine so $^G$brightly,

We are the $^D$stars, we are the $^{A7}$stars,

So see us $^D$shine.

We are the stars of peace and harmony,

We are the stars of love and light,

We are the stars that shine so brightly,

We are the stars, we are the stars,

So see us shine.

---

NOTE TO TEACHER

Sing a song during each lesson and do a Quietly Being exercise each day.

---

Cooperation

## COOPERATION LESSON 2
# Water to the Horse

**Teacher Preparation:** Have plastic buckets available or ask the children to bring in a safe container that is available in most homes in your area.

Discuss the following Cooperation Reflection Point: Cooperation is working together toward a common goal. Ask:

- What does that mean? (Define goal.)
- What if there is no water in the trough for the horse? What would our goal be? ("Yes, that's right—to bring it some water.")

Say, "Cooperation is very important. For example, if there was no water in the trough for the horse and there were no farmers around to help, how could people cooperate to fill the trough?" Explore the different solutions the children propose, and then say, if not already suggested, "Suppose we had buckets?"

## Activity

Outside, use a small plastic swimming pool for the pretend horse trough and ask the children to see how they could fill it by using the containers. If it is a warm day, you may consider having water in their containers. While they may try a few other methods, conclude the activity by asking them to stand in a line and pass each container from hand to hand as a person at the beginning fills the containers.

*—Contributed by Dominique Ache*

Cooperation

## COOPERATION LESSON 3

# Stories

Tell stories about cooperation. One favorite is "The Enormous Turnip," in which one person wants a huge turnip growing in the ground. Many finally help by pulling together and are hence successful in getting the turnip out of the ground.

The children can draw pictures about the stories they are told.

## COOPERATION LESSON 4

# Cooperative Building

## Activity

Small teams of children can share and enjoy cooperation by building houses out of Lego bricks, blocks or milk containers. Put the Lego bricks or blocks on a table or on the floor and encourage children with the words, "Come, let us build a house together for all of us."

The adult should provide encouragement and perhaps some help in the beginning by building a stable foundation, if necessary. Some children who are not used to cooperating or sharing may need a little more monitoring and specific praise for little bits of patience, waiting and sharing.

## COOPERATION LESSON 5
# Cooking Together

Cooking together in small groups with a teacher can be an enjoyable experience of working together. If no cooking facilities are available, the children can make sandwiches or fruit salads. Point out how we can all do different things but work together to get one thing done.

## COOPERATION LESSON 6
# Painting a Butterfly

**Preparation:** Depending on the ages and skills of the children, the teacher may wish to do the following in advance: Stick together four sheets of paper or use one large piece of paper. Fold it in half, and draw and cut out a large butterfly.

## Activity

Four children cooperatively paint two wings on one side of the butterfly. The other four children at the opposite half are to copy the painted wings exactly. (It is a good idea to let the older and more mature children do the copying work.)

COOPERATION LESSON 7

# Cooperative Games

## Activity

Play cooperative games with the children. Ask them to find a partner, sit down, hold hands, and then help each other stand up at the same time but without letting go of the other person's hand. Then sit down again without letting go of each other's hands. Try it again!

Perhaps when they want to go outside to play, they must get there cooperatively. With a ribbon, tie the left ankle of one child to the right ankle of another or ask three or more children to keep hold of one ribbon. Applaud as each team reaches the doorway.

## Discuss/Share

Afterward, at circle or sharing time, discuss what made walking that way easier.

Say, "The more we observe, decide what is needed, and cooperate with affection, the better we achieve the task."

COOPERATION LESSON 8

# More Cooperative Games

## Activity

Introduce the activity: Tell the children they will be expected to cooperate in two ways.

As they will be holding a ribbon and must not let go, they must cooperate by paying attention to how they walk. If they are careful and cooperate, they will discover how to walk easily! Another way they must cooperate is by tossing or kicking the ball so that the other person can reach it. Everyone wins when the ball keeps going back and forth.

This activity may be better outside on the grass if the weather is good. Get three or four children to hold on to the ribbon (as noted in the previous lesson). Provide a balloon or ball and let them play tossing it back and forth. As with the other tasks, affirm positive comments and fun.

**Another Activity:** Get two children to hold on to a ribbon and ask them to team up with two other children who are also holding on to another ribbon. Their task is to kick a ball back and forth between teams.

 ## Discuss/Share

- What helped you walk when you were holding on to a ribbon with someone else?
- What things do you like to hear when you are trying to do something together?
- What things make you feel good when you cooperate?

Acknowledge their responses. If they have not mentioned the following, ask if they would like to hear some other examples. Act out the following, adding comments you may have heard. Say:

| With a negative voice tone: | With a positive voice tone: |
|---|---|
| "No, not that way, stupid." | "Let's try it this way." |
| "That's a little better." | "Good!" |
| "You missed it again." | "Good try." |

Cooperation

COOPERATION LESSON 9

# Can I Help You?

Discuss the idea of a Cooperation Table.

## Activity

Create a Cooperation Table. Allow children to take turns at the table, for little ones perhaps just a few minutes at a time. The child taking a turn as the "Cooperative Person" is to help each person who comes to the table. Set up an age-appropriate task. For example, for three-year-olds, the children could go to the Cooperation Table when they want glitter for their project.

## Discuss/Share

Say, "One person at a time will be able to help at the Cooperation Table. I was thinking that we all might want cooperation sometimes." Ask:

- Is there anything you want cooperation with? (You might get real problems to solve—a great opportunity!)
- Do we want a clean room/playground/_____?
- How can we cooperate to make that happen?

If there is a problem that needs solving, ask for the children's cooperation. Perhaps cooperation is needed in cleaning up the room or accompanying one child at recess, break or throughout the day. Ask for volunteers. Affirm their affectionate and helpful cooperation.

Cooperation

## Activity

Draw a picture of yourself cooperating at school.

**Continue:** If convenient for the teacher, continue to allow the children to take turns at the Cooperation Table at other times in the next few days. During discussion time, take up the social skills of asking for help and giving help in a positive and appropriate way.

---

**Lesson 10**

COOPERATION LESSON 10

# Puzzles

## Activity

Assign small groups of children to work together on an activity, such as creating a large puzzle. Positively affirm that they are sharing and working together.

If a large puzzle is not available, the teacher can make thick black lines with a marker to simulate a puzzle on the backs of large pictures that the children made. The children can then cut the pieces out and put the picture back together. The teacher can make the picture into a few pieces or many pieces, depending on the age of the children.

## Discuss/Share

• What helps us to make working together feel like cooperation?

Responses may be: Saying please, asking me nicely to do something, sharing, telling me I did a good job, etc. Positively acknowledge these positive social behaviors and list them on a board or poster.

Cooperation

COOPERATION LESSON 11

# Puzzles Continue

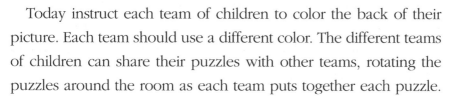

## Activity

Today instruct each team of children to color the back of their picture. Each team should use a different color. The different teams of children can share their puzzles with other teams, rotating the puzzles around the room as each team puts together each puzzle.

Then mix all the pieces from all the teams together and begin the game of discovering which piece belongs to which puzzle. Ask all the children to be cooperative in making all the puzzles whole again. Have a good time.

Remind the children to use cooperative language and skills, and provide positive reinforcement when they do so!

COOPERATION LESSON 12

# Cooperation at Home

## Discuss/Share

- How are you cooperative at home?
- How do you help _____?

## Activity

Ask each child to draw a picture of himself or herself cooperating at home.

Cooperation

**Lesson**
# 13

## COOPERATION LESSON 13
# Cooperative Mural

**Introduction:** "Before, several of you worked together to make large pictures and butterflies. Now the whole class will work together in cooperation by making one large picture. We call that a mural. Today I want you to decide what you would like to make on your mural."

## Discuss/Share

- What kinds of things would be in a big picture of a peaceful world?
- What kinds of things would be in a big picture of a cooperative world?
- Which one would you like to do?
- Would you like to use children in the pictures, or bears, or _____?
- What would you like them to do?
- Shall we have teams of children cooperate in making the mural? We will need some people to paint the sky, some to paint nature and some to paint people doing things. Who would like to _____?

Divide the children into smaller teams with specific responsibilities. Each team can work on its part. The teacher may wish to provide younger children with pre-drawn forms, which they can cut out and paint. They can then stick these onto the mural rather than paint directly on the mural. Monitor and help as needed, positively affirming cooperative behaviors.

Cooperation

COOPERATION LESSON 14

# Cooperative Mural Continues

Continue with the mural.

COOPERATION LESSON 15

# Cooperation Builders

## Discuss/Share

- When you are working on something, what things do you like to hear that make you want to cooperate?
- What things make you feel good when you cooperate?

List what the children say. Help small teams put those words onto paper and decorate them. Then add them to the mural.

COOPERATION LESSON 16

# Cooperative World Race

**Teacher Preparation:** Cut a large piece of paper into a circle, and then cut that into pie-shaped wedges—as many as half the number of children in your class.

## Discuss/Share

- What quality or value do you think is needed for a peaceful, cooperative world?

Cooperation

## Activity

After the whole class discusses the above topic, divide the children into pairs. Instruct each pair to decide on one value or quality the children agree is important for a peaceful, cooperative world. Give each pair a piece of the pie-shaped wedge of paper, and ask the children to write their one value on that piece of paper.

Go outside to a grassy area or a playground for a three-legged race. Each pair carries its value paper. The teacher, standing at the finish line, collects each pair's value as the pair arrives. The recipe for your peaceful, cooperative world is completed when every pair arrives.

*—Contributed by Marcia Maria Lins de Medeiros*

COOPERATION LESSON 17

# Cooperation Review

Begin with the Filling Up with Love exercise.

## Discuss/Share

Ask the children what they enjoyed most about the lessons on cooperation and what they learned.

## Activity

Paste your pie-shaped wedges of paper back into the circle, everyone focusing on his or her best cooperative behavior.

End with a song.

Cooperation

# SEVEN

# Honesty Unit

# 7. HONESTY UNIT

Reflection Points . . . . . . . . . . . . . . . . . . . . . . . . . . 141

Objectives . . . . . . . . . . . . . . . . . . . . . . . . . . . . . 142

**HONESTY LESSONS**

Lesson 1    A Mirror . . . . . . . . . . . . . . . . . . . . . . . 143

Lesson 2    The Emperor and the Flower Seeds . . . . . . 145

Lesson 3    Stories. . . . . . . . . . . . . . . . . . . . . . . . . 145

Lesson 4    Only the Truth Is Spoken Here . . . . . . . . 146

Lesson 5    One Minute of Courage . . . . . . . . . . . . . 147

Lesson 6    Lost and Found . . . . . . . . . . . . . . . . . . . 149

## Honesty Reflection Points

♦ Honesty is telling what really happened.

♦ Honesty is telling the truth.

♦ When I feel honest, I feel clear inside.

♦ When I am honest, I can learn and help others learn to be giving.

Honesty

## Honesty Unit

### GOAL: To increase appreciation of honesty.
### OBJECTIVES:

❏ To become aware of an example of being rewarded for honesty by acting out the story, "The Emperor and the Flower Seed."

❏ To talk or draw about feelings when someone breaks a promise.

### GOAL: To increase understanding about honesty.
### OBJECTIVES:

❏ To talk about one of the Honesty Reflection Points, such as honesty means telling the truth or honesty means telling what really happened.

❏ To be able to distinguish between telling the truth and not telling the truth when the adult demonstrates by saying what he or she is doing with an object.

### GOAL: To build honesty skills.
### OBJECTIVES:

❏ To play a game in the classroom in which the children find someone's favorite toy, report it missing and return it to the owner.

❏ To tell a real story or share something that really happened when interviewed on the pretend television.

# Honesty Lessons

Honesty Reflection Points help define the value. The points can be used as the first focus point during values time or can be a discussion point as part of language arts. Allow the children the opportunity to share their experiences about that value.

For five- through seven-year-olds, the teacher can choose to use some of the words and sentences as content for reading, spelling and writing. As the students continue with the unit, they can create their own Honesty Reflection Points. They can then draw or write those or make up short stories.

---

HONESTY LESSON 1

## A Mirror

**Explain:** "In the next four weeks (or whatever length of time), we're going to learn about honesty." Ask:

• Who can tell me about honesty?

Accept their responses.

**Demonstrate:** Say, "Honesty means telling the truth, telling what really happened. I'm going to do a few things and then tell you the truth about what I did." Model several actions, telling the children what you did after each one. For example,

Pick up two blocks and say, "I picked up two blocks."
Pick up a doll and say, "I picked up the doll."
Say, "My name is _____."
Hug Maria and say, "I hugged Maria."

Honesty

Tell the class what honesty means again—telling what really happened, telling the truth. Ask each child to practice the same thing with a partner.

Tell the children that not being honest means not telling the truth, not telling what really happened. "I'm going to do something, and not tell you the truth about what I did." Demonstrate what you said. For example, pick up a book and say, "I picked up a table." Ask, "Did I tell the truth? No." Pick up a doll and say, "I picked up a truck." Ask, "Did I tell the truth? No." Tell the class what honesty means again—telling what really happened, telling the truth.

## Activity

Practice Telling the Truth with a Mirror. Little children, ages three and four, like this game. Provide a mirror. Describe the arm movements you are making and what you see when you look in the mirror. Allow the children to do the same. This allows language development as well as a lesson on what honesty means.

—*Contributed by Encarnación Royo Costa*

---

### NOTE TO TEACHER

Include a song during each lesson and do a Quietly Being exercise every day.

---

Honesty

## HONESTY LESSON 2

# The Emperor and the Flower Seeds

**Read the story:** "The Emperor and the Flower Seeds" (Appendix). Discuss the story, asking comprehension questions.

## Activity

Arrange for the children to make props for acting out the story, such as a crown for the king, a pot for Serena, a little box and flowers.

The next day: Retell the story, and as you do so, allow half the class to act it out. Retell the story, and as you do so, allow the other half of the class to act it out.

## HONESTY LESSON 3

# Stories

Tell your favorite story about honesty—perhaps reading from a children's book or recounting a personal story from your childhood.

## Discuss/Share

- Do you like it when someone tells the truth?
- One example of telling the truth is keeping your promises. I want you to think of someone who always tells the truth. How do you feel about him or her?

Say, "When people tell the truth and are honest, we feel we can trust them. That feels good."

Honesty

- Do you know someone who does not tell the truth?
- How do you feel when someone breaks a promise?

If they share stories about people breaking their promises, acknowledge their feelings, such as, "Yes, it is very disappointing when people don't keep their promises."

> ### NOTE TO TEACHER
>
> If some of the children share stories about parents not keeping promises, you may wish to say: "Sometimes adults forget how important it is to keep promises to children. Parents love their children very much—sometimes they forget to keep their promises because they are so busy thinking about other things."

## Activity

Draw a picture about something they talked about.

**Lesson 4**

HONESTY LESSON 4

# Only the Truth Is Spoken Here

Conduct a daily interview for several days during sharing time, using an imaginary television (a cardboard frame is usually sufficient). Write "Only the Truth Is Spoken Here" above the area where the interview takes place. Initially, the teacher can act as the interviewer. Later, as the children observe how interviewing is done, they can take turns as the interviewer. The children can bring in something to share for the interview, or the teacher can ask simple questions.

*—Contributed by Dominique Ache*

Honesty

NOTE TO TEACHER

If you are working with four- and five-year-olds who are having difficulty distinguishing between "real" and "pretend," you may wish to tell a couple of real versus pretend stories. Make your pretend stories very obvious, and then ask them, "Was that real or pretend?" For example, "One day I was walking down the street and I saw Mohammed and his mother," versus "One day I was walking down the street, and all of a sudden I saw a big green foot! It was as big as a house!"

HONESTY LESSON 5

# One Minute of Courage

Only do this unit if there are children in the group who are having difficulty with honesty and they are five years or older. Be light about this topic, and remember that most children do not have a firm grasp on the difference between reality and fantasy until they are about four or five years old.

Start by bringing up for discussion why people sometimes do not tell the truth. "We've been talking about honesty." Ask:

• Why do you think people sometimes don't tell the truth?

"Yes, often it is because they don't want to get into trouble or because they don't want somebody to get mad at them or be disappointed in them. We all want people to love us. It sounds like that is what happens with us sometimes, too. . . . So we

Honesty

sometimes try to hide what happened so we don't get into trouble and so they don't get mad or disappointed."

- But what happens when people find out we lied?

"Yes, that's right. They get even madder and more disappointed, and we get into even more trouble. And although adults may not look so clever sometimes, usually they can figure out the truth fairly well! And if we lie once, they may not trust us to tell the truth another time." Ask:

- Do we want people to trust us?

"It's important to tell the truth so that our relationship has trust. When there's lots of truth in the relationship, we feel safe and very loved. But it sometimes takes courage to tell the truth when, for instance, something goes wrong, or when we did something we weren't supposed to do, or when we didn't do something we were supposed to do. But let's see if we can practice telling the truth all morning."

Check in with the children at lunch and ask them to continue practicing the rest of the day. Positively reinforce their efforts. If it looks as if a child is not going to tell the truth, use the reminder, "One minute of courage . . ."

Invite the children to draw a picture or write a story about their own experiences. They could also make up simple poems about honesty. For example:

> *I am honest,*
> *I am true.*
> *When I'm not,*
> *I am blue.*

Honesty

HONESTY LESSON 6

# Lost and Found

## Discuss/Share

- How would you feel if you lost your favorite toy?
- How would you feel if someone found your toy and returned it to you?
- How would you feel if you lost your lunch money (or something equivalent)?
- How would you feel if someone saw you drop your money and returned it to you?
- How would you feel if we all worked very hard and then someone stole all our money?

Acknowledge the children's feelings and responses. Acknowledge that it is not nice for someone to do that.

Say, "Some people are not honest. Some people are very greedy. What do greedy people say? They say, 'It's all for me! It's all mine!' And they take what belongs to others."

## Activity

Say, "Let's have a lost-and-found game today." Instruct each child to make a picture of his or her favorite toy on a colored piece of paper. Then play a game in the classroom in which half the children close their eyes while the others hide their colored pieces of paper.

The children who had their eyes closed now open their eyes and search the room to find one of the hidden drawings. As each

*Honesty*

one finds a drawing, he or she is to come up to the teacher and say, "Teacher, look what I found!" The teacher can thank each child and then ask the class whose it is. The "finder" can then hand it to the owner.

Ask the children if they would rather have someone find their toy and keep it. Enjoy their responses. Then allow the other half of the class to do the same game.

Discuss the following Honesty Reflection Points:

◆ When I feel honest, I feel clear inside.
◆ When I am honest, I can learn and help others learn to be giving.

Draw a picture of what an honest person does.

# EIGHT

# Humility Unit

# 8. HUMILITY UNIT

Reflection Points. . . . . . . . . . . . . . . . . . . . . . . . . . 153

Objectives . . . . . . . . . . . . . . . . . . . . . . . . . . . . . . 154

**HUMILITY LESSONS**

Lesson 1   Humble Cartoon Characters . . . . . . . . . . 155

Lesson 2   Sharing Cartoon Characters. . . . . . . . . . . 157

Lesson 3   Staying Happy While I Listen . . . . . . . . . . 157

Lesson 4   Staying Happy While I Listen Continues. . . 159

Lesson 5   Sharing and Listening. . . . . . . . . . . . . . . 159

   Song   My Wings . . . . . . . . . . . . . . . . . . . . . . . 160

Lesson 6   This Friend Helps Us Wait Our Turn . . . . . 160

Lesson 7   Wings of Respect and Humility . . . . . . . . 162

Lesson 8   Wings of Respect and Humility . . . . . . . . 162

## Humility Reflection Points

- ♦ Humility is staying easy and light inside.
- ♦ Humility goes together with self-respect.
- ♦ Humility is when I know why I'm wonderful, but I don't brag or show off.

Humility

♦ A humble person can stay happy inside while listening to others.

♦ Humility means I behave well while I wait my turn.

## Humility Unit

### GOAL: To increase knowledge about humility.
### OBJECTIVES:

❑ To be able to talk about two of the Humility Reflection Points.

❑ To name a superhero or cartoon character who has the balance of self-respect and humility.

❑ To be able to demonstrate or identify the difference between a bragging tone of voice and a tone of voice with humility and self-respect.

❑ For each child to make two "wings" with their qualities.

### GOAL: To build social skills which have the balance of self-respect and humility.
### OBJECTIVES:

❑ To interact with others without bragging or bullying.

❑ For each child to name three of his or her own positive qualities and to listen patiently as a classmate shares three of his or her qualities.

❑ To think about how to stay happy while we listen to others.

❑ To learn how to interrupt politely and to deal politely with interruptions.

# Humility Lessons

Humility Reflection Points can be used to help define that value. The points can be used as the first focus point during values time or can be a discussion point as part of language arts. Allow children the opportunity to share their experiences about that value.

For five- through seven-year-olds, the teacher can choose to use some of the words and sentences as content for reading, spelling and writing. As the students continue with the unit, they can create their own Humility Reflection Points. They can then draw or write those or make up short stories.

HUMILITY LESSON 1

## Humble Cartoon Characters

Lesson

1

Begin with the Respect Star exercise.

Explain: "In the next four weeks (or whatever length of time), we're going to learn about humility."

Share the following Humility Reflection Points:

♦ Humility is staying easy and light inside.
♦ Humility goes together with self-respect.

Say, "It's a little bit hard to define humility. It's a feeling of staying easy and light inside. It goes with self-respect, with knowing your good qualities. If you know your good qualities, then you can keep your power inside—you can feel good inside. People who have self-respect and humility don't need to brag or show off."

Humility

## Discuss/Share

- Can you think of someone who has self-respect and humility? Perhaps one of your favorite cartoon characters?

## Activity

Children and teachers can pick some favorite fantasy characters who work toward good in a humble, non-bragging way. These could be Simba from the movie *Lion King* when he was an adult, or perhaps Batman, Wonder Woman or Superman. You may also choose examples from legends or fairy tales with which the children are familiar. Demonstrate the following:

1. First practice saying something with self-respect and humility. For example, Superman might say, "I know I have been gifted with an ability to fly from one part of the world to another. It is important that I use my abilities for doing good deeds, not evil. I enjoy helping people."

2. Then practice saying something with a bragging tone. For instance, Superman might say, "I can fly, I can leap over tall buildings, I get a lot of attention because I am always doing things to help people. I don't know what this world would do without me."

The adult could use the Superman example or any example with which the children would relate easily. Ask:

- Was there a difference in my tone of voice when I said those things?
- Which one made you feel better about _____?

Ask the children to pretend they are a character and describe what makes them feel proud about what they do. Ask a few of them to demonstrate the two voice tones (bragging and humble).

Humility

## Activity

Ask the children to draw and color a picture of their favorite cartoon character and to write in a thought bubble something that character might say with self-respect. The teacher can help the younger students to write.

---

NOTE TO TEACHER

Include a song during each lesson and do a Quietly Being exercise every day.

---

HUMILITY LESSON 2

# Sharing Cartoon Characters

## Discuss/Share

Invite one child at a time to stand by the teacher and share his or her picture. They can practice each of the voice tones if they like. Some favorite characters could be posted on the wall.

---

HUMILITY LESSON 3

# Staying Happy While I Listen

Discuss the following Humility Reflection Points:

♦ Humility goes together with self-respect.
♦ A humble person can stay happy inside while listening to others.

Humility

Sometimes people get grumpy when they hear good things about others—but that's only because they are afraid they aren't as good!

- Do you ever feel that way? (If "yes," ask "When?")

Acknowledge their feelings. Add, "It helps to remember that everyone can be wonderful—all at the same time. If someone else is good, you can be good, too!" Ask:

- What helps us stay happy while we listen?
- Shall we make up silly poems about that?

> Others are good,
> And so am I!
> When we've listened to each other,
> We'll have some pie!

> He is smart,
> And so is she,
> And all us smart ones
> Can sit in a tree!

> I can feel good,
> Even when you brag,
> Because I know,
> You're not a cad!

## Activity .

Make up silly poems.

## HUMILITY LESSON 4

# Staying Happy While I Listen Continues

## Activity

Ask the children to illustrate their poems with a drawing. Then invite each child to share his or her poem and drawing with the class as all students in the class stay happy while listening.

## HUMILITY LESSON 5

# Sharing and Listening

Say, "Today we're going to practice two Humility Reflection Points."

♦ Humility goes together with self-respect.
♦ A humble person can stay happy inside while listening to others.

## Activity

Ask the students to remember three things they like about themselves. (This was done during the Respect unit and is a good review.) Ask each student to share those three things with a partner. The partner is to listen and repeat what was said. They each get a turn to share and to listen/repeat back. Positively reinforce the children for speaking in a confident (not bragging) voice and for active listening behavior.

*Humility*

Begin learning the song:

## My Wings

$^E$One wing makes me strong,

And the $^B$other makes me light.

$^{B7}$When I use both of them,

I can $^E$fly just right.

$^E$One wing is self-respect,

The $^B$other humility.

$^{B7}$With both of them,

$^E$I'm as happy as can be.

$^E$I have two wings

To help me fly.

$^A$Oh, can you see!

I know how to fly!

$^B$Come on, fly with $^E$me!

## HUMILITY LESSON 6

# This Friend Helps Us Wait Our Turn

Say, "Humility is a wonderful friend to have. When Humility is your companion, you know you are lovable and capable and unique. Humility is a friend because it helps you stay steady and feel patient inside. Humility likes you and others when you wait your turn. Sometimes waiting our turn is hard because we want something as soon as we desire it. Humility is our friend because it helps us behave well and reminds us to give love to ourselves while we wait our turn."

Humility

Positively reinforce the children for waiting and for being patient and enjoying themselves while they wait. Gradually taper off the reinforcement as the social skills of waiting and delaying gratification are learned. Occasionally, however, do notice when they are demonstrating humility. "You have the balance of self-respect and humility! You are not interrupting each other. You are patiently waiting your turn to speak!"

## Activity

Ask, "Who would like to demonstrate someone not waiting his or her turn?" Ask three children to demonstrate someone interrupting two other children, and then ask the same three children to demonstrate waiting patiently. Ask:

- How do you feel when you are interrupted rudely?
- How can you interrupt someone politely?
- If you know someone wants to interrupt, how can you let the other person know you know they are there and will get to them in a minute?

Reinforce their good ideas and ask them to demonstrate. Write down their suggestions on the board. Ask for another three volunteers to do the same.

**Reinforce:** During the next couple weeks, positively reinforce the children's polite methods of interrupting or dealing with interruptions. Refer to the suggestions they made. Some of the children may wish to make a poster of their suggestions.

Practice the "My Wings" song.

Humility

HUMILITY LESSONS 7 AND 8

# Wings of Respect and Humility

**Awareness:** When we have both self-respect and humility, it is easy to stay happy and maintain our power inside.

Take two days to make the wings.

1. Making the wings. Help the children make two wings for themselves—one for Self-Respect, one for Humility. Take a piece of paper large enough to hang from their arms, from the upper arm to the wrist. Cut it out so when it is folded over the arm (or in half), it hangs down twelve inches at the upper arm and twenty-four inches at the wrist. Cut scallops on the bottom edge when the paper is still folded.

2. Decorating the wings. The children can decorate the wings with words or symbols that represent their qualities and help them maintain their power. For instance, for the Self-Respect wing, they might write SMART, FRIENDLY, HELPER. For the Humility wing, they might write LIGHT, EASY, SWEET, HAPPY.

3. Decorating the child. The wings should fold over the child's arms like an envelope. Staple the lower edges of the paper wings. Use safety pins to pin the wings to the clothing of the child at the upper side of the upper arm.

## Song and Dance

Ask the children to sing the "My Wings" song and do a simple circle dance, moving their arms up and down. You may want to

Humility

teach them a dance step before they put on their wings, or it may be more fun helping them invent a dance once they have their wings. Toddlers can simply circle one way and then the other way, flapping their wings while they sing.

Humility

# NINE

# Tolerance Unit

# 9. TOLERANCE UNIT

Reflection Points. . . . . . . . . . . . . . . . . . . . . . 168
Objectives . . . . . . . . . . . . . . . . . . . . . . . . . . 168

**TOLERANCE LESSONS**

Lesson 1   The Interview. . . . . . . . . . . . . . . . . . 169
Lesson 2   A Tree of Treasures. . . . . . . . . . . . . 171
    Song   Friends Make the World Go Round. . . . 171
Lesson 3   Josh the Dragon . . . . . . . . . . . . . . . 173
Lesson 4   A Rainbow . . . . . . . . . . . . . . . . . . . 173
Lesson 5   Stories from a Variety of Cultures . . . . . 174
Lesson 6   Dances and Foods from a
           Variety of Cultures. . . . . . . . . . . . . . 175
Lesson 7   Liking Myself—Even When I Make
           a Mistake . . . . . . . . . . . . . . . . . . . 175
Lesson 8   A Store. . . . . . . . . . . . . . . . . . . . . 176
Lesson 9   Tolerance Review . . . . . . . . . . . . . . 176

Tolerance

## Tolerance Reflection Points

♦ We are all unique and have something valuable to offer and share.

♦ Tolerance is accepting others and appreciating differences.

♦ Tolerance is accepting myself, even when I make mistakes.

♦ Tolerance is accepting others, even when they make mistakes.

## Tolerance Unit

### GOAL: To increase tolerance through appreciating uniqueness and different cultures.

### OBJECTIVES:

❏ For each child to identify ways in which he or she is unique, and to feel happy, proud or appreciative of that difference.

❏ To understand that it is okay to be unique—or "different."

❏ To understand that all races and cultures are important for the beauty of the human rainbow.

❏ To hear stories from three different cultures.

❏ To make cut-out figures in traditional dress to put up on the rainbow.

❏ To sing a rainbow song.

### GOAL: To increase tolerance through compassion.

### OBJECTIVES:

❏ To understand that people often feel sad when others are mean to them or exclude them because they are different.

**GOAL: To build tolerance/acceptance/patience with the self.**

**OBJECTIVES:**

❏ To not be frustrated when making a small mistake on classwork.

❏ For children with sufficient language ability to state the rule, "It's okay to make a mistake; all I have to do is correct it."

# Tolerance Lessons

Tolerance Reflection Points can be used to help discuss this value. The points can be used as the first focus point during values time or can be a discussion point as part of language arts. Allow the children the opportunity to share their experiences about that value.

For five- through seven-year-olds, the teacher can choose to use some of the words and sentences as content for reading, spelling and writing. As the students continue with the unit, they can create their own Tolerance Reflection Points. They can then draw or write those or make up short stories. The teacher can share one point for several days.

TOLERANCE LESSON 1

## The Interview

**Explain:** "In the next few weeks we are going to learn about tolerance. One of the meanings of tolerance is accepting everyone and appreciating our differences." Ask:

Tolerance

- What would the world be like if everyone accepted every-one else?

Acknowledge their responses and confirm, "Yes, we would have a peaceful world." Continue, "One of the Tolerance Points is: We are all unique and have something valuable to offer and share. So we are going to start understanding tolerance by look-ing at how each one of us is unique and has something valuable to offer and share."

- What is unique about each one of you?

If the children cannot generate differences, illustrate a few dif-ferences with the questions below:

- What is the name of your mother?
- What is your favorite cartoon character?
- What is your favorite story?
- How many have grandparents who speak a language dif-ferent from the one we are speaking now?

Be interested and celebrate the differences.

## Activity

If there is a small group, ask the children to share a couple of ways in which they are unique. The group could make a televi-sion frame out of cardboard, and the children can share from behind the frame. Lead the children in applauding each child. For a larger group, have them share one uniqueness.

*—Contributed by Dominique Ache*

Tolerance

> **NOTE TO TEACHER**
>
> Include a song during each lesson and do a Quietly Being exercise every day.

TOLERANCE LESSON 2

# A Tree of Treasures

**Lesson 2**

## Activity

To accept "the universe" of each other, invite each child to bring from home something he or she likes. Or, depending on the circumstances, ask each child to make a small drawing of one of his or her favorite things—perhaps a toy, an activity or a food. Draw a tree on a large sheet of paper and allow the children to put their small drawing on the tree.

Talk about how each one is unique, and how wonderful the tree is because it has so many different types of treasures.

*—Contributed by Encarnación Royo Costa*

Begin to learn the song:

## Friends Make the World Go Round

Chorus:     <sup>Bb</sup>Friends make the <sup>Eb</sup>world go <sup>Bb</sup>round

<sup>Eb</sup>Friends make the <sup>Eb</sup>world go <sup>Bb</sup>round

Friends make the <sup>Eb</sup>world go <sup>Bb</sup>round

<sup>Eb</sup>Friends make the world go <sup>Bb</sup>round

<sup>Eb</sup>They'll bring you a <sup>F</sup>smile

When <sup>Eb</sup>you've got a <sup>Bb</sup>frown

<sup>Eb</sup>Give you a <sup>F</sup>laugh

When <sup>Eb</sup>you're feeling <sup>Bb</sup>down

<sup>Cm</sup>Friends come in <sup>F</sup>red, yellow

<sup>Cm</sup>Black, white and <sup>F</sup>brown

Yes, <sup>Bb</sup>friends make the <sup>Eb</sup>world go <sup>Bb</sup>round

<sup>Eb</sup>Friends make the world go <sup>Bb</sup>round

Verse:     <sup>Bb</sup>A new kid moves <sup>Am dim</sup>in one day.

<sup>Bb</sup>I ask, would you <sup>Am dim</sup>like to play?

We <sup>Bb</sup>swing on the <sup>Am dim</sup>monkey bars.

<sup>Bb</sup>Make believe we <sup>Am dim</sup>touch the <sup>Bb</sup>stars.

We talk about <sup>Am dim</sup>things we like.

<sup>Bb</sup>Flying kites and <sup>Am dim</sup>riding bikes.

She <sup>Bb</sup>said I'm glad <sup>Am dim</sup>I met you.

I <sup>Bb</sup>said that I <sup>Am dim</sup>was glad <sup>Bb</sup>too.

*(Repeat chorus.)*

Verse:     <sup>Bb</sup>Eat ice cream and <sup>Am dim</sup>play some more,

<sup>Bb</sup>Roam around like <sup>Am dim</sup>dinosaurs.

<sup>Bb</sup>Make some funny <sup>Am dim</sup>faces too,

<sup>Bb</sup>Acting like we're <sup>Am dim</sup>at the <sup>Bb</sup>zoo.

But <sup>Bb</sup>then we (both) have <sup>Am dim</sup>to go home,

<sup>Bb</sup>So I call her <sup>Am dim</sup>on the phone.

Ask <sup>Bb</sup>if she can <sup>Am dim</sup>play again.

<sup>Bb</sup>It's so much fun <sup>Am dim</sup>making <sup>Bb</sup>friends.

*(Repeat chorus two times.)*

—*Contributed by Max and Marcia Nass*

Tolerance

## TOLERANCE LESSON 3
# Josh the Dragon

Begin with the last lesson's song.

**Story:** Read "Josh the Dragon" to the children (Appendix).

## Activity

Ask the children comprehension questions about the story, and then ask them to draw a picture or act it out.

## TOLERANCE LESSON 4
# A Rainbow

Sing a song about a rainbow.

**Explain:** Compare a rainbow to human beings. The human race is like a rainbow in that there are many different cultures and races. We are all human beings. We all have eyes, a nose, a mouth, hands with fingers and feet with toes. But we speak different languages and come in different shapes and colors. Some eyes are oval and some eyes are round. Some skin is whiter and some more brown. Each culture and each race is important and unique—just like each color of the rainbow.

## Activity

Ask the children to paint a rainbow as part of the room's decoration. Or ask them to cut out colored paper for a rainbow.

Tolerance

## TOLERANCE LESSON 5

# Stories from a Variety of Cultures

For the next several sessions, read stories from three different cultures, including your own. Include stories of different cultures existing in your own country.

Point out the qualities of each culture and the similar themes in each story. After you have read each story, ask the children to give examples of qualities. "In the story about _____ _____, how was love shown? In the story about _____, how was courage shown?"

## Activity

If the class made a large rainbow (previous activity), the teacher can put the name of the culture or race in one arc of the rainbow, adding the qualities the children pointed out from the story. That can be done on different days after each story is read. The children can make pictures or paper dolls of the people from the different stories and place them around the rainbow. If possible, draw the people in their traditional dress.

## TOLERANCE LESSON 6
# Dances and Foods from a Variety of Cultures

Look at the rainbow and the variety of cultures the class has studied. Revisit each culture, learning a dance, singing a song or cooking a food from each one. Perhaps some parents could help.

## TOLERANCE LESSON 7
# Liking Myself— Even When I Make a Mistake

**Introduction:** Talk about tolerance for the self—accepting and liking myself, even when I make a mistake. It is important to have tolerance and patience when mistakes are made. You might want to tell them a rule: "It's okay if you make a mistake; just try to correct it. We don't need to become angry or sad or to feel bad. Sometimes we do become angry at ourselves, or we feel sad or bad. That's because we don't know the rule: It's okay if you make a mistake; just try to correct it." This is a rule the adults can help the children use throughout the year, especially when the children are experiencing difficulty with a task.

—*Contributed by Thomas R. Bingham, Program for Affective Learning*

Read a story from the children's culture about something or someone with a tolerant and patient attitude.

Tolerance

TOLERANCE LESSON 8

# A Store

You may want to set up a store on a nearby table and have three- and four-year-olds "shop" for a certain number of objects. Use cards to designate the number of objects. The teacher would write, for instance, the number five on the front of the card and may want to include the correct number of circles underneath. The objective is for the children to bring back to the teacher the correct number of objects for the number on the card in their hand. Usually children will not be able to do this correctly the first time. Teach the numbers with lots of love and the attitude that they are learning from their mistakes. (Make sure it is challenging but can be achieved after a few tries.)

TOLERANCE LESSON 9

# Tolerance Review

Enjoy doing the dances or songs again.

Review the cultures you have studied by asking the children what they liked about the unit on tolerance: the rainbow, the stories they remember, what they learned and what they liked doing.

**Root Sentence:** Ask the children to stand in a circle and finish the sentence, "Human beings are one family because _____
_____."

Tolerance

# TEN

# Simplicity Unit

# 10. SIMPLICITY UNIT

Reflection Points. . . . . . . . . . . . . . . . . . . . . . . . . . . 179

Objectives . . . . . . . . . . . . . . . . . . . . . . . . . . . . . . 180

**SIMPLICITY LESSONS**

Lesson 1   Simple Pleasures . . . . . . . . . . . . . . . . . . 181

Lesson 2   Appreciating Trees. . . . . . . . . . . . . . . . . 181

Lesson 3   Conservation . . . . . . . . . . . . . . . . . . . . 182

Lesson 4   Appreciating Nature . . . . . . . . . . . . . . . . 183

Lesson 5   Making Our Playthings . . . . . . . . . . . . . . 184

Lesson 6   Mother Earth . . . . . . . . . . . . . . . . . . . . 185

Lesson 7   Making Number and Letter Books . . . . . . . 185

## Simplicity Reflection Points

♦ Simplicity is natural.

♦ Simplicity is learning from the Earth.

♦ Simplicity is beautiful.

♦ Simplicity is using what we already have and not wasting the Earth's material.

Simplicity

## Simplicity Unit

**GOAL: To increase understanding about simplicity.**
**OBJECTIVES:**

- ❏ To identify simple pleasures and simple things they enjoy.
- ❏ To enjoy playing with simple things, such as cardboard boxes.
- ❏ To make their own number or letter book.

**GOAL: To build appreciation for nature and be introduced to conservation.**
**OBJECTIVES:**

- ❏ To understand that conservation is using what we have and not wasting the earth's resources.
- ❏ To decide to do one or two things to help nature, and to carry through on the ideas.

# Simplicity Lessons

Simplicity Reflection Points can be used to help define that value. The points can be used as the first focus point during values time or can be a discussion point as part of language arts. Allow the children the opportunity to share their experiences about that value.

For five- through seven-year-olds, the teacher can choose to use some of the words and sentences as content for reading, spelling and writing. As the students continue with the unit, they can create their own Simplicity Reflection Points. They can then draw or write those or make up short stories.

## SIMPLICITY LESSON 1

# Simple Pleasures

**Explain:** "In the next few weeks we are going to learn about Simplicity. Simplicity means valuing what is natural, what is simple. Today I want you to think of things that are natural, things that you don't have to buy. For example, a simple pleasure in life is enjoying a pretty flower, or getting a hug from someone who loves you."

- What simple pleasures do you enjoy? (Another example could be hearing your mother sing.)
- What are simple things you enjoy doing?

## Activity

Draw or paint a picture of a simple pleasure in life, or a simple thing you enjoy.

---

**NOTE TO TEACHER**

Include a song during each lesson and do a Quietly Being exercise every day.

---

## SIMPLICITY LESSON 2

# Appreciating Trees

## Discuss/Share

Say, "Two of the Simplicity Reflection Points are: Simplicity is beautiful and, simplicity is natural. One thing that is beautiful and

Simplicity

natural is a tree." Talk about the beauty of nature and the importance of trees. For example, "Trees give us wood for our houses, paper to write with, paper bags to carry things in, oxygen for breathing and wood for fires so we can keep warm. Trees provide shelter for animals, too. They give humans food, too." Ask:

- What fruits come from trees?
- What else do trees give? (Food for animals, materials to make boxes, etc.)

## Activity

Ask the children to pretend they are different kinds of trees. Go out to the playground or a park to enjoy the trees and collect different types of leaves. Or make leaves with paper and crayons or paint. Each child then takes a turn stating what type of tree he or she is and what this tree gives to animals and humans. The children may want to wave their leaves around as they explain. Ask, "As trees, do you have a message to give to humans?"

Lesson

3

SIMPLICITY LESSON 3

# Conservation

Introduce the following Simplicity Reflection Point: Simplicity is using what we already have and not wasting the Earth's material.

Explain: One way we can be simple is by using what we already have and not wasting the Earth's material. Nature gives generously to us, and we must be careful so there will always be enough.

## Discuss/Share

Talk about conservation. "Conservation means we don't waste what nature gives us. We plant one or two trees when we use one, and we reuse the resources they give. How can we conserve the things that come from trees in the classroom (paper, boxes, sticks)?" Ask the children to suggest ways they can conserve in the classroom, and with the teacher's guidance, pick one or two to do.

Make up a song or poem about conservation. The following poem points out that one way of conserving is not needing to have one of everything!

> It's okay to be simple,
> It's okay to be kind.
> I love the Earth—
> I don't need
> one of every kind!

---

SIMPLICITY LESSON 4

# Appreciating Nature

Lesson

4

Let's think about water for a minute.

- What do we use water for?
- Do we need water every day?
- Where does water come from? (From the ocean to clouds, from rain to rivers to us.)

Simplicity

- What happens if the water in the rivers is dirty (gets polluted)?
- How can we help the water stay clean?
- What other natural things are beautiful?

Continue the conversation with the natural things they bring up, ending with the note that nature provides us with simple but very important things.

## Activity

Do a task to help the environment, such as picking up trash from a river or planting flowers.

SIMPLICITY LESSON 5

# Making Our Playthings

**Awareness:** When we play with simple things, we can be creative and use our imagination. We are also recycling by using those things again.

## Activity

Place before the children during playtime cardboard boxes collected from the grocery store or fruit stand. Children at ages three and four will often start playing spontaneously with the boxes, sometimes two or three squeezing inside one box and using another box as a lid, saying, "This is our house." Or, they can pretend it is a train and sing, "The wheels on the train go round and round." They can make a tower, etc.

## SIMPLICITY LESSON 6
# Mother Earth

Discuss the following Simplicity Reflection Point: Simplicity is learning from the Earth.

- What can we learn from Mother Earth?

Read a story. There are many wonderful stories about Mother Earth and the lessons she teaches. Enjoy one of those with the children. Have them act out the story or draw pictures when you are done.

## SIMPLICITY LESSON 7
# Making Number and Letter Books

**Awareness:** We can create our own learning material.

## Activity

Ask children to create their own number or alphabet books. For three- and four-year-olds, the teacher will need to trace the numbers one through five or one through ten, each number on a separate piece of paper. The children can then put the corresponding number of happy faces on those sheets of paper. Alphabet books can be made with pictures of objects starting with that letter.

Simplicity

# ELEVEN

# Unity Unit

# 11. UNITY UNIT

Reflection Points . . . . . . . . . . . . . . . . . . . . . . . . . . . 189
Objectives . . . . . . . . . . . . . . . . . . . . . . . . . . . . . 190

## UNITY LESSONS

Lesson 1    Stories . . . . . . . . . . . . . . . . . . . . . . . . . 191

Lesson 2    Musical Squat . . . . . . . . . . . . . . . . . . . . 192

Song    Let Us Clap Together . . . . . . . . . . . . . . 193

Lesson 3    Pulling Our Car . . . . . . . . . . . . . . . . . . . 193

Lesson 4    Someone New in Our School . . . . . . . . . . 194

Lesson 5    One Goal . . . . . . . . . . . . . . . . . . . . . . . 195

## Unity Reflection Points

♦ Unity is harmony in the group.

♦ Unity is doing something together at the same time.

♦ Unity is working together with a shared goal.

♦ Unity makes big tasks seem easy.

♦ Unity is fun and makes us feel like a family.

## Unity Unit

### GOAL: To experience unity in the classroom.
### OBJECTIVES:

❏ To experience unity as they sing the clapping song.

### GOAL: To increase knowledge about unity.
### OBJECTIVES:

❏ To learn about animals that practice unity.
❏ To be able to talk about two Unity Points.

### GOAL: To practice unity.
### OBJECTIVES:

❏ To learn it is important to extend to other children the feeling they are accepted.
❏ To join together with the common goal of pulling a child in
the toy train.
❏ For the class to come to a consensus in choosing a common
project and to work together on that goal.

# Unity Lessons

Unity Reflection Points can be used to help define that value.
The points can be used as the first focus point during values time
or can be a discussion point as part of language arts. Allow the
children the opportunity to share their experiences about that
value.

For five- through seven-year-olds, the teacher can choose to
use some of the words and sentences as content for reading,

spelling and writing. As the students continue with the unit, they can create their own Unity Reflection Points. They can then draw or write those or make up short stories.

---

UNITY LESSON 1

# Stories

**Explain:** "In the next few weeks we are going to learn about unity."

Discuss the following Unity Reflection Points:

♦ Unity is harmony in the group.
♦ Unity is working together with a shared goal.

**Stories:** Tell one story every day for several days. Tell stories about the animals which practice unity, such as geese, dolphins and elephants. Find story books about animals or tell true stories. For example, there are many true stories about dolphins saving humans. In one, a group of dolphins swam many miles, pushing a man on a raft who was lost at sea. The dolphins took turns pushing the raft with their noses. They were united in their goal of saving the man. When some dolphins were tired, others would take over. They kept swimming together, and when others were tired, the ones who were more rested would push again. They rotated for many, many miles. They pushed the raft until it was close to a little village by the sea and the man could swim safely by himself to the shore.

Unity

Elephants have many similarities to humans. They have a seventy- to eighty-year life span. They mate for life and love their children very much. When the elephants live in a jungle and are threatened by a tiger or lion, the large elephants form a circle around the baby and young elephants. The parent elephants face outward in the circle so they can guard their children and keep them safe. If a tiger comes, they grab it with their trunks and toss it. The elephants are united; they act together with a shared goal.

## Activity

Draw a picture about each story told, or act it out.

---

### NOTE TO TEACHER

Include a song during each lesson and do a Quietly Being exercise every day.

---

Lesson
2

UNITY LESSON 2

# Musical Squat

Discuss the following Unity Reflection Point: Unity is doing something together at the same time.

## Activity

This is a fun game of unity. The goal is to have everyone sit down when the music stops without breaking the circle.

Directions: Play some music and ask the children to walk in a circle, facing in the direction they are walking. When the music stops, every person in the circle must sit down on the lap of the person behind him or her. They do this by clasping the waist of the person in front and gently lowering themselves onto the lap of the person behind. (For four-year-olds, this is quite easy!) If the circle does not collapse, then everyone has won.

Sing the following with everyone doing the motions as they sing.

### Let Us Clap Together

DLet's all clap together, Atogether, Dtogether,
Let's all clap together, Aclap, clap, Dclap.
DClap, clap this a way
AClap, clap that a way
DClap, clap this a way
AAll day Dlong.

*Continue the song, substituting the words (and actions):*

Stamp
March
Skip
Walk
Twist
Hop
Sit Down

UNITY LESSON 3

# Pulling Our Car

Lesson
3

Sing the "Let Us Clap Together" song.
Discuss the following Unity Reflection Points:

Unity

♦ Unity is harmony in the group.

♦ Unity is fun and makes us feel like a family.

## Activity

Make cars from large cardboard boxes, and attach a rope for pulling. The cars can be painted or decorated with bits of paper. The children can then give each other rides by five or six pulling one passenger at a time.

Lesson

# 4

UNITY LESSON 4

# Someone New in Our School

The adult shares that part of unity is making everyone feel that he or she belongs. "Sometimes we are really comfortable in a class or a group because there is a feeling that everyone knows me and loves me. So sometimes, when someone new comes along, people do not make extra effort to make that person feel a sense of belonging. In unity, we can be open to change and enjoy all the new children who come to our group." Generate a discussion with the children by asking:

• How might a new child feel coming to a new school?

• How did you feel the first time you came to preschool (or kindergarten, etc.)?

• What did you like other people to say and do when you came?

• What else can you do to make new children feel like they are welcome and belong?

They might suggest sharing a snack, saying hello, smiling, telling the new child their name or asking if he or she wants to play. Encourage them to come up with their own ideas.

UNITY LESSON 5

# One Goal

Talk about unity as working together to make something happen which everyone wants to happen—that's called a goal. The adult may want to ask them what goal they have. Or, depending on the age of the children, the adult could offer a choice of two or three group projects that the children could adopt as goals. The projects might be planning a party, planting a small garden outside or making something. Ask the children to come to a consensus on a project they would like to do. Point out that unity is thinking together about what you want to create, and feeling enjoyment because you are doing it together.

Sing some of the songs the children learned previously, such as "Each One of Us Is Beautiful" or "The Star Song."

# APPENDIX

## Item 1: Peace

## The Star Story

**By Diana Hsu**

Once upon a time, there was a lovely, bright, shining family of Peace Stars. The head star of the family was the smiling Sun Star. He was a very special star. He had so much love for all the other stars, and he would send loving beams of light to them. The stars liked this very much, and so they were peaceful and happy. The Sun Star was happy that they were happy, and he smiled day and night. He loved to look at his Peace Star children.

The children of Earth were pleased that all the stars were happy—they liked to look up at the stars and see them sparkle. The children of Earth liked to see the Star children play with each other, sometimes shooting across the sky. Sometimes the stars would play with the Earth children. But one day the friendly stars in the sky saw two Earth children fighting with each other. "Oh," one of the Peace Stars said to another, "Let's go quickly and help these two children before they hit each other!" As fast as lightning, they flew to the two children and sent them peace beams and friendly beams. They even tickled their noses with their beams so the children had to laugh.

In the meantime, the Fearless Star had noticed what was happening on Earth, and since he was without fear, he and the Courageous Star flew down to the children. They introduced themselves, and the Courageous Star said: "I am called the most courageous star in the Star family because I never quarrel or fight with anyone. Not to quarrel or fight is the most courageous thing to do."

By now, the Loving Star and the Laughing Star had noticed the group, and they focused their bright beams on the children, so the children forgot their anger.

The big Helper Star and the Patient Star had also arrived. "Children," said the Helper Star, "isn't it lovely how all these stars have come down to Earth to help you? Shall I tell you a secret?"

"Yes, yes!" exclaimed the children.

"The greatest secret," said the Helper Star, "is patience. Look at the Patient Star! Nothing can upset him. He is always patient with others. Everyone loves him."

"That's right," said the Cautious Star, "If you are careful about how you treat others and you treat them with respect—why, then it's easy not to hurt or be hurt by others. Then you don't need to fight."

By now, almost all the Star children had arrived on Earth, and they were joined by many, many Earth children. "We want to be like the Stars," said the Earth children. Suddenly they saw something very bright shining in the sky. It was the Brightest Star, together with the Happy Star and the Laughing Star. The Brightest Star beamed at the children, and the Laughing Star had such a funny laugh that the children simply couldn't help but laugh as well.

"Let's have a good time!" sang the Happy Star, and they started to play and sing. The Stars brought yummy treats. It was the best party anyone could imagine. All were happy. They danced, played, ate and laughed. "This is the best party ever!" everyone agreed.

Then it happened! Nobody had noticed the arrival of the Quiet Star, but then she spoke: "The great Sun Star has sent me to you," she said softly and sweetly. "Every party has to come to an end, and you are to go home now."

The children on Earth had also been thinking about going home, for it had become quite dark. They hugged the stars good-bye. One of the Peace Stars said softly to the children, "Know that we are always here for you—even in the daytime when you can't see us. Just picture us in your mind, and you will feel our beams of love and peace." And the Star children beamed brightly at the children

and then flew back to the great Sun Star. It was a lovely sight. As the Peace Stars flew higher and higher, they sent bright beams and loving thoughts to the children below.

All the Peace Stars sent peace, and each Peace Star sent his or her own special quality as well. The Patient Star sent patience. The Laughing Star sent a happy laugh. The Quiet Star sent soft, quiet beams. The Loving Star sent lots and lots of loving thoughts. The children on Earth watched happily and waved to the stars. "Come back soon," they cried, and then returned home.

Do you think that the children and the Peace Stars ever met again? Do you think that we can become as peaceful, happy and loving as the Star children?

## Item 2: Respect

# Lily the Leopard

## By John McConnel

Lily the Leopard thought there was something gravely wrong with her. Unlike all the other leopards she knew, her spots were not black but pink. It would not have been so terrible if the other leopards had accepted her. But the other leopards would not accept her. In fact, even her own family shunned her. Her mother had cried upon seeing her baby daughter covered in pink spots, and her father and her two brothers, Julian and Ricky, were ashamed to have such a strange-looking leopard in the family. The other leopards in the neighborhood ignored her, laughed at her and sometimes poked at her, just because her spots were a different color

from their spots. Sometimes she felt afraid and sad, and other times she got very angry. So she decided that she would stay alone most of the time. She spent her days lying in a bush, watching the other leopards frolic about. Even when they would occasionally call Lily to come out to play, she would remember their past insults and would growl low in response to their invitation.

It was not her fault she had pink spots! She was different and could not help it. Often she wondered why the other leopards didn't understand. She had done her best to rid herself of her pink spots. Lily tried scrubbing and washing them away. She tried bleaching them. Once she even painted them black, but the pink soon shone through the paint. Nothing worked. After a while, she realized that she was stuck with them. What else could she do?

One day, after four young cubs were teasing her, Lily decided to run away from home. She had had enough. She ran off into the jungle as fast as she could. Lily ran for hours, just stopping to rest now and then and to wipe the tears from her eyes.

Eventually, she came to rest in a clearing and fell asleep. She was awakened by the soft touch of a tongue on her nose. As she looked up, she saw the most amazing sight. Before her stood a great big leopard with bright green spots! Lily was so surprised by what she saw that she blinked twice just to make sure she wasn't dreaming. She had often had dreams of other leopards with different colored spots, but she never imagined that there actually were such leopards. The great leopard with bright green spots told her his name was Lenny and asked her what she was doing so far from home. As he spoke, he seemed to glow with confidence and happiness. His eyes were filled with kindness, and so Lily felt safe and soon found herself telling her story.

Lenny quietly listened to her story. When she finished, he gave her a warm hug and helped her dry her eyes. He then smiled at her and said, "What you need is some self-respect."

"I do?" asked Lily. "What's that?"

"Self-respect means liking yourself, even when others do not," said Lenny. "It means appreciating all the special things about yourself."

"There's nothing special about me except these pink spots, and I hate them!" she cried. "I am so strange and ugly. I wish I was never born!"

"Don't be silly," said Lenny. "You're very special. There is no one like you in the whole world, and I can see that you have many good qualities." Lenny paused for a moment. He seemed to be thinking. "I have an idea," he said.

"Let's make a list of all the things you like about yourself."

"Okay," said Lily, brightening a little. She sat for a few moments thinking and then said: "Well, I'm kind and caring, and I try to be friendly. I help my mom and dad and I'm very loving . . ." Lily paused for a moment, her voice trailing off. Lenny nodded his head eagerly in order to encourage her. Lily felt safe again and so she continued. "I have beautiful gold eyes, and I'm a very fast runner. I'm brave and strong and . . ."

Just then Lucy the Leopard appeared with Laura the Leopard. Lucy was covered with blue spots and Laura in purple spots. As soon as they saw Lily, they were delighted. They smiled grandly and leapt into the air. "What a lovely leopard you are, and what a beautiful coat you have!"

"Thank you," Lily replied, smiling as she remembered there was much more to her than met the eye. Suddenly, she felt much better.

"It's okay to be different," she thought. "In fact, I think my spots are rather pretty! If other leopards do not like me because of my pink spots, that's because they don't know better. I'm okay. I'm glad I'm unique."

Lily spent a few more hours playing with her newly found and brightly colored friends. But as the sun began to set, Lily began to think about her family. They might be worried about her, she thought. Lily waved goodbye to Lenny and Lucy and Laura. She promised them, however, that she would visit them again soon, and off she went. As she walked home, she watched the sun set. For the first time, she noticed the many brilliant colors in the sky. The sky was pink, blue, green, purple and orange. "How beautiful," she thought. "I wonder why I never noticed all those colors before."

When Lily finally arrived home, her mom and dad and two brothers ran to meet her. As they came closer to Lily, they noticed there was something different about her. She seemed to shimmer and glow. She held her head high as she trotted forward and smiled at them warmly. "She is really quite beautiful," they thought. And they wondered why they had never noticed that before.

## Item 3: Love

# The Happy Sponges

### By Teresa Garcia Ramos

Once upon a time there was an ocean where some very happy sponges lived. It was not just any ocean, but an ocean of love. That was the reason for their happiness—they were always full of love.

One day, one of the sponges approached the edge of the ocean. It decided to play with the waves and roll up to the beach. At last it reached the beach. And what did it see? A girl sat on the sand. Her name was Marion.

She did not seem to notice the beautiful ocean or the clear blue sky, but just looked down. She didn't seem very happy. The sponge was surprised to see such a sad face on such a sunny day. The sponge greeted her: "Hello, girl! What's up? You seem unhappy. I have always heard that boys and girls constantly smile."

Marion answered almost reluctantly, "No. Many people feel sad." She looked at the sponge carefully and said, "I am so surprised to see a such a happy sponge. I haven't seen such a happy face. Why are you so happy?"

The sponge answered, "It is very easy. Since I live in the ocean of love, sponges like me constantly absorb love. We share that love with others. And when any sponge is distracted and forgets to take love, then some accidents happen. Only then do some of the sponges get sad or angry."

Marion sat up a little straighter and asked eagerly, "What do you do then?"

"Well," answered the sponge, "then all the other sponges go to the sad or angry sponge. We fill ourselves with love, then we squeeze ourselves and give love to the sad or angry sponge. It's easy!"

Marion said, "You are my friend, sponge. I think I would like to be like you. Do you think that it's possible for boys and girls to fill with love and be as happy as you?"

The sponge answered, "Of course!"

And she said, "But I am not a sponge! I am a girl. How can I do it?"

The sponge said, "It doesn't matter, you just have to believe in love. You are like a sponge because you can fill yourself up with love, and you can give that love to others."

Marion exclaimed with joy, "That's great! I'm going to practice!" She took a big breath and practiced filling up with love in her mind. She smiled and said, "It is true! I feel happier already!"

The sponge said, "You see, it is easy. Regarding love, we are all the same."

## Item 4: Responsibility

# The Seed

### Based on a story by Encarnación Royo Cuesta

Once upon a time there was a boy named Juan. He was six years old and lived in a small house next to a river at the foot of a mountain with his parents and a sister a little older than he. One day, when coming back from school, he heard a voice that cried, "Help, help! Please, help me!"

Juan listened and searched until at last he was standing in a spot where the voice seemed loudest. He looked around but could not see anybody. The voice said, "Look down. I'm here." Much to his surprise, the voice seemed to be coming from a brown seed about the size of his thumb. This seed was lying on a stone.

Juan asked, "What's wrong?" A sad voice from the seed said, "I am so glad you came along. I have been sitting and sitting on this stone for ever so long. Several other people came by, but they did not stop. I was afraid no one would stop."

"Why, I'm surprised they didn't stop!" said Juan. "Sometimes people get so busy they forget to listen," he explained politely.

The seed said, "I've been sitting here for a long time. I know there is something I must do, something I must know. But I'm not sure what it is. Do you know my purpose?"

Juan was surprised at such a question. He looked at the seed very carefully and slowly said, "Well, I understand why you are sad if you do not know your purpose. That is very important. But don't worry! I will take you with me and I will look for the right place for you to live. I will try and help you figure out what you need. Then you will discover by yourself, little by little, your purpose. I do know that everyone can give something important to the world. I bet you can, too."

And that is how Juan found the seed the size of his thumb and ended up taking it home. When he arrived home, he talked to his mother, and she told him what seeds need. The next morning, he made a hole in the ground on the sunny side of the house. He carefully loosened the soil and gently placed the brown seed inside. Then he covered the hole with soil and watered it.

But the following day, the seed began to cry again, saying, "Help! I am alone again and everything is dark! Why has Juan left me here?"

When Juan heard the seed crying, he apologized for forgetting to explain why he did what he did. Then Juan said, "Don't worry and don't feel sad. It is necessary that you have some time to prepare for what you need to do. I will come to visit you every day, and I will take care of you. I will give you water every day, and you will see that in a little time, you will grow. Be happy inside and know that you are preparing to serve. Soon you will notice that you are growing little roots. And soon a stem will start to grow upward. That will be called your trunk."

Then the seed asked the boy, "Did you also have to take time to prepare?"

"Of course," answered Juan. "Everyone has to prepare—that's part of being responsible. Now I am preparing at school. I know I'm smart and I know how to think and learn. Be patient. It takes time to prepare, and everything prepares in its own way."

Just as Juan had said, he came to visit the seed and give it water every day. The seed grew and grew. Soon a stem started to peek through the ground, and two little leaves began to unfold. The sun warmed it and gave it light. It grew stronger and taller, and it became apparent that the seed was growing into a strong, wonderful tree!

The boy and the tree continued to talk. After several years, flowers began to blossom all over the tree, and little green balls grew from them. These changed in color from green to blush and finally to exactly the color of apricots.

The now larger boy carefully picked the first ripe apricots and praised the tree. "You have grown into a strong apricot tree, and your apricots are delicious."

So this small seed, with the care of a boy who knew how to be responsible, became something very important. The tree said to Juan, "Thank you, friend, for taking care of me with so much love. Now I know my purpose!"

Juan answered, "You are very, very important. As a tree you give us clean air, shade, beauty, and even fruit to eat. I am your friend, but you are a friend to the whole world."

And that's how this tale ends.

## Item 5: Happiness

# The Heart School

### By Diana Hsu

Marc lived in a small town not far away from here. He lived with his mother in a small house. The house was surrounded by grassy fields and huge trees, and the school he went to was within walking distance. Marc sometimes thought how lucky he was not to have to live in one of those large cities, where there were hardly any parks in which he could play with his friends.

Besides playing outside a lot, Marc liked to spend time in his room. He was always busy. He liked to collect stamps from all over the world, play with his cars and buses, Legos and airplanes. But one thing he did not like very much was going to school.

One Monday morning, as he started to walk to school, he somehow felt this would be a very special day. It was a bright day, the sun was shining, the birds were singing, beautiful butterflies were flying by and the air was filled with the sweet fragrance of colorful flowers. He felt as if this would really be the most special day in his whole life. Marc stopped walking. He lay down on the grass and closed his eyes. As he started to enjoy this, he relaxed. Then suddenly, with his eyes still closed, he saw himself walking ahead and reaching a heart-shaped house. As he came nearer to this house, he could feel that this was a very special place. Now he could read the letters above the door:

## The School for Loving Children

As if by a magnet, Marc was drawn to look through the window and . . . "Ooohh!" he exclaimed, ". . . what a wonderful world!" He saw a classroom decorated with light-colored paintings of butterflies, rainbows, flowers and happy children playing. He saw mobiles of birds, stars and hearts. The curtains and furniture were brightly-colored, and in the windows were transparent pictures and collages through which the light was shining like a rainbow.

Marc saw the teacher and her children sitting in a circle on the carpet. He looked at the faces of the children. They were sparkling with happiness. And then his eyes were drawn to one particular child. "It's me! It's really me!" he thought. "I am one of these happy, loving children, shining with so much joy!" Marc was surprised that suddenly he felt so light—it was as if his heart was saying, "I am a happy, loving child!" And then suddenly the school disappeared. Marc got up from the grass and with light steps continued onward to school, wishing his own school was like the one he had just seen.

The next morning, Marc could hardly wait to reach that same spot on the grass again. He wanted to see that heart school again. He searched and searched, but the school was nowhere to be found. Was it all a dream? Somehow he knew it was not. He felt a sudden disappointment. "I feel . . . I feel . . . I want to cry!" thought Marc.

"Marc, Marc," he heard someone whisper. He looked up, and floating down from the sky, seated on a giant rainbow-balloon, was a smiling Golden Bear. As the balloon landed, the heart-shaped school appeared behind him.

"Hello," said the Golden Bear. Taking Marc's hand, he whispered gently, "Come and see yourself, Marc." And as he looked through the window, he

could see himself standing with the others, holding hands in a circle and listening to the teacher.

"Maria, can you please play the flute?" the teacher asked.

When Maria started to play her flute, they all started to dance. What fun they were having! And Marc noticed that no one was pushing, breaking the circle, kicking or being nasty to the others, and no one was left out. The room was filled with magical sounds.

As Marc continued to watch, the children and the teacher were moving from one activity to another without any unkind words being spoken. A little while later, Marc saw himself drawing and sharing his pencils with the others. The teacher, with a smiling face and kind eyes, was going from child to child, listening quietly while each child was telling her about his or her drawings. After all the drawings were finished, Marc saw the children packing away their things and then decorating the walls. Each child was admiring the work of the others. What harmony there was!

The children then sat in groups at their tables and took out their arithmetic books. Everyone quietly listened to the teacher, who spoke in a clear, soft voice, explaining what needed to be done.

Marc watched as the teacher looked over the shoulder of the boy who looked like him and said, "Well done, Marc! All your sums are correct, and your work is neat."

Marc looked up at the Golden Bear. "How can that be me? I am not good at arithmetic. My work is not neat and the teacher is seldom pleased with me!"

The Golden Bear just smiled and held Marc's hand tightly. "Just watch, just watch!"

When Marc looked up through the window again, he saw himself confidently reading aloud to the class. Much to his surprise, everyone was listening eagerly. "Look at that, I can do it, I can do it!" he said to the Golden Bear. "I can read without feeling scared and stumbling over the words!"

"Of course you can!" said the Golden Bear. He seemed to know Marc well. What a wonder!

Then the children sat down in a circle to have their lunch. As the food was passed around, Marc could see himself waiting patiently. No one was pushing and no one was calling out, "Me first! That's mine! Give that to me! I am not your friend anymore." And no one snatched the food away from anyone else.

Marc saw himself asking his friend, "Would you like a piece of cake?"

"Thank you," replied his friend, and he offered Marc some fruit and nuts.

After lunch, Marc noticed that the children seemed happy helping one another. No one laughed at others' mistakes. Everyone seemed to be friends—and happy to see one another succeed!

When it was time to go home, the teacher said, "I look forward to seeing you again tomorrow." As Marc saw himself leaving, the teacher smiled and said, "Goodbye, Marc."

Marc turned to the Golden Bear, "How can I be like that?"

The Golden Bear just smiled and said, "If, from your heart, you really want to change . . . just wait and see . . . just wait and see! Goodbye, Marc." And off the Golden Bear floated.

## STOP READING HERE!

## CONTINUE READING HERE TOMORROW.

When it was bedtime, Marc thought about how wonderful it would be to dream of the heart-school again. He closed his eyes and waited, but no heart-school appeared. He waited some more and nothing happened. "Oh well," he thought. "It was nice while it lasted." But then, right in front of him, slowly and gently, the Golden Bear floated down to the foot of his bed, holding onto his rainbow-balloon. Marc gave him a big smile and said, "It's you! I was wondering whether I would ever see you again!"

"Hello!" said the Golden Bear. "I was listening to the thoughts of your heart. You want to be the happy you, the real you. Everyone likes to be loved by all."

"Yes," said Marc slowly, "it's like magic how you seem to know everything!"

"Well," said the Golden Bear, "it is not as difficult as you think. Shall I help you a little? I am going to show you a secret. Look, here are two boxes. Read what is written on them."

### HAPPY      UNHAPPY

The Golden Bear took the Unhappy Box and asked, "What do you think is in this box?"

"I don't know," replied Marc, "but it can't be anything good!"

The Golden Bear opened the Unhappy Box and took out four cards.

"What's written on them?" Marc asked the Bear impatiently.

"Guess first!" said the Golden Bear.

"Mm, mm . . . I don't know!" responded Marc.

The Golden Bear looked amazed. "But you do know what makes you unhappy, don't you?"

"Well, yes," Marc started slowly, "when I push or hurt others, or if they push or hurt me, that makes me unhappy."

"That's right!" said the Bear. "Now I will read what is written on the cards: pushing and kicking others, speaking harsh and hurtful words, thinking 'I can't do it,' and being impatient."

"Is that what makes me really unhappy?" asked Marc. "When I hurt others or when I am impatient?"

"Yes, that's right," said the Golden Bear, "and then everyone is unhappy with you as well."

"Please take the cards from the Happy Box now," Marc asked the Bear.

The Bear took four cards from the Happy Box and read them to Marc. "Be patient, say only kind words, help others, and always have good thoughts about yourself and others."

"Is this the secret of being happy?" Marc asked.

"Yes," explained the Bear, "and when you are happy, that is when you are the real you! That is why it is so easy to change. I'll help you!" he added, seeing the look on Marc's face.

"Listen very carefully now," said the Golden Bear. "Tomorrow, when you pack your school bag, open the Happy Box and take out one card. Read the message carefully, and when you're in school, just do what the card says. If you follow it, it will work! I'll see you tomorrow evening to hear how your day went."

And swiftly the Golden Bear lifted off and floated away with his rainbow-balloon, waving and smiling as Marc waved and smiled back.

The next morning, Marc got out of bed early and got ready quickly. This was going to be the first day of happiness at school. When everything was ready, Marc took a card out of his Happy Box. As he was taking the first card, it seemed that he could hear the voice of the Golden Bear. "What have you picked, Marc? Tell me."

Astonished, Marc looked around but could not see the little Bear. "Strange," he thought, but he really had heard his voice. "Tell me what you have picked," Marc heard again.

"Okay, I took a card and it says, 'Do everything with a *smile*,'" Marc said out loud.

"Oh, that is wonderful," Marc could hear the Bear saying. "It is easy! Tell me, what are you going to do?"

Marc started slowly, "I will . . . I will . . . I will say good morning to every-one with a smile. If someone is unfriendly, I will smile instead of hitting him or saying something mean. If my teacher tells me to write neater, I will smile at her instead of getting upset, and . . . "he finished in a rush, "anyway, I will do everything with a smile today."

"Okay," smiled the Golden Bear, "see you this evening!"

When Marc came home from school that day, he could hardly wait to see the little Bear to share all the news with him. Marc looked around and soon the Bear appeared, floating down on his rainbow-balloon.

"I could see your happy face from afar," the Bear said.

"Yes, Bear, oh, it was a wonderful day! I did everything exactly as I told you this morning and guess what? Not only did I smile," Marc said proudly, "but others started to smile, too, and seemed to get along better with each other."

"Well done!" said the Bear.

"Yes," added Marc. "And Hugo wanted to kick me. But I just stood there fearlessly and smiled . . . and you know what happened then? He forgot about kicking me! He sort of looked at me in a funny way and turned around and walked away. I think he forgot about kicking altogether today. It is amazing!" exclaimed Marc. "Oh, I am looking forward to taking another card from the Happy Box tomorrow. Will you come tomorrow to hear about my happy day?"

"Yes, I will come! Good luck for tomorrow, and be strong!" said the Bear. As the Golden Bear was flying off with his balloon, Marc ended the day happily. Oh, how exciting life can be when you discover something new!

The next morning, Marc got up early again and picked his card for the day from the Happy Box. "Little Bear, can you hear me? Today I've picked, *be patient*. I've thought about what I will do. Shall I tell you?

"I will let others go first.
I will not rush to finish my work too quickly.
(I always want to finish first, so that I get praised.)
I will help others patiently and will wait happily when others are speaking.
I will listen carefully to what my teacher is telling me.

"Oh, I can hardly wait to get to school today!" said Marc.
Marc had a long day at school. His face was not so happy when he got home. He finished his dinner slowly and went to bed early.

"Oh, I almost forgot, the little Golden Bear wanted to come," thought Marc. It was as if the Bear heard his thoughts, for he was suddenly standing right in front of him.

"It wasn't so easy today, was it?" gently asked the Bear, looking at Marc's face.

"Well, do you know what happened? I did everything as I said this morning, but I forgot one thing, and that was to be patient with myself," said Marc. "I rushed to finish quickly, and because of that, I dropped some paint and it splashed all over the floor! And only then did I remember that I wanted to be patient with myself. Bear, it wasn't pleasant at all! You know why? Not only did I drop the paint, but when one of my classmates started to laugh at me and made fun of me, I said some hurtful words to him. And then I felt awful afterward."

"Cheer up, Marc! You've only just started to become the happier you! That needs a little time, and these things happen sometimes. Just try not to make the same mistake again," the Bear said in his most encouraging manner.

"I'm glad to hear that, Bear. It makes me feel a lot better," said Marc.

With a big smile the Bear opened the Unhappy Box and turned to Marc, saying, "Write down your unhappiness about the spilled paint and about being angry with your classmate, and slip it into the Unhappy Box. Then close the box, and it is over and done with! As easy as that! What's past is past. There's no need to worry or to be upset about it. Try to understand what went wrong, tell yourself that you won't make the same mistake again, and then forget it completely. Remember only what went right today and what made you happy, and think about what you are going to do tomorrow to be happy." The Golden Bear paused a moment, and then he added, "Tomorrow you will try again and you will succeed, and that's a promise!"

Marc suddenly felt very light and full of confidence. "Yes, tomorrow I will try again and succeed! Oh, I can hardly wait until tomorrow to take the next card!" Marc laughed happily as the Bear grabbed the string of his rainbow-balloon and got ready to float away. The Bear looked at him. His eyes were full of love and hope. Suddenly Marc felt that his heart, too, was filling with love and hope. He could feel the great confidence the Bear had in him. "He believes in me and I know it will work! With the help of the little Bear I will be victorious and become the real me, happy and loving!"

Dear children, now that you have just listened to this story, how do you think it will end? Share your ideas with others in your class.

Okay, listen now to what happened. Day by day, Marc would take a card from his Happy Box and think about how to use it at school. Most of the time he was good and successful, but sometimes he would make a mistake. When he made a mistake, he would not get upset or worry. Instead, he would try to understand what went wrong, write it on a piece of paper, and tell himself he would not let the same mistake happen again. Then he would slip the paper into the Unhappy Box and close the lid and forget about it!

And so, day by day, Marc grew stronger and stronger and happier and happier. The amazing thing was that after a while the other children in the class changed, too, because he was such a good example to them and his growing happiness worked like magic! Do you want to know what happened in the end?

Gradually, all the children in the class discovered the secret about the Happy Box and asked every day, "Marc, what are you doing today to become happier?"

Marc would share with them what was written on the card. Do you know what happened next? They joined in. In a short time all the children were becoming happier and happier, until in the end all the children in the class were treating each other like friends and being loving and caring toward each other.

IT WAS JUST LIKE MAGIC!

## Item 6: Honesty

# The Emperor and the Flower Seeds

Long ago, in this very kingdom, there lived an emperor who loved nature. Anything he planted burst into bloom. Up came flowers, bushes and even big fruit trees, as if by magic! Of everything in nature, he loved flowers most of all, and he tended his own garden every day. But the Emperor was very old, and he needed to choose a successor to the throne. Who would his successor be? And how would the Emperor decide? As the Emperor loved flowers so much, he decided that flowers would help him choose.

The next day, a proclamation was issued: "All men, women, boys and girls throughout the land are to come to the palace." The news created great excitement throughout the land.

In a village not far from here, there lived a young girl named Serena. Serena had always wanted to visit the palace and see the Emperor, and so she decided to go. She was glad she went. How magnificent the palace was! It was made from gold and was studded with jewels of every color and type: diamonds, rubies, emeralds, opals and amethysts. How the palace gleamed and sparkled! Serena felt that she had always known this place. She walked through the palace doors into the Great Hall, where she was overwhelmed by all the people. It was so noisy. "The whole kingdom must be here!" she thought.

There then came the sound of at least a hundred trumpets, announcing the arrival of the Emperor. All fell silent. The Emperor entered, clutching what looked like a small box. How fine he looked—so noble and elegant! He circled the Great Hall, greeting every person and presenting something to each one. Serena was curious about the small box. "What is inside?" she wondered. "What is he giving to everyone?"

At last, the Emperor reached Serena. She curtsied and then watched as the Emperor reached into the small box and presented her with a flower seed. When Serena received the seed, she became the happiest girl of all.

Then the sound of trumpets filled the Great Hall once more, and all became silent. The Emperor announced: "Whoever can show me the most beautiful flowers in a year's time will succeed me to the throne!"

Serena left for home filled with wonder over the palace and the Emperor, clutching the flower seed carefully in her hand. She was certain she could grow the most beautiful flower. She filled a flowerpot with rich soil, planted the seed carefully and watered it every day. She couldn't wait to see it sprout, grow and blossom into a magnificent flower!

Days passed, but nothing grew in the pot. Serena was worried. She transferred the seed into a bigger pot; filled it with the best quality, richest soil she could find; and watered it twice a day, every day. Days, weeks and months passed, but still nothing happened. By and by the whole year passed. Finally spring came, and it was time to return once more to the palace. Serena was heartbroken that she had no flower to show the Emperor, not even a little sprout. She thought that everyone would laugh at her because all she had to show for the whole year's effort was a pot of lifeless soil! How could she face the Emperor with nothing?

Her friend stopped by on his way to the palace, holding a great big flower. "Serena! You're not going to the Emperor with an empty pot, are you?" said the friend. "Couldn't you grow a great big flower like mine?"

Serena's father, having overheard this, put his arm around Serena and consoled her. "It is up to you whether you go or not," said her father. "You did your best, Serena, and your best is good enough to present to the Emperor."

Even though she felt reluctant to go, Serena also knew she must not disregard the Emperor's wishes. Besides, she also wanted to see the Emperor and the palace again. And so Serena traveled once more to the palace, holding the pot of soil in her hands.

The Emperor was happy to see the Great Hall filled with his subjects, all proudly displaying their beautiful flowers, all eagerly hoping to be chosen. How beautiful all the flowers were! Flowers were of every shape, size and color. The Emperor examined each flower carefully and thoroughly, one by one. Serena, who was hiding in a corner with her head bowed down, wondered how he could choose, since they were all so lovely. Finally, the Emperor came to Serena. She dared not look at him. "Why did you bring an empty pot?" the Emperor asked Serena.

"Your Majesty," said Serena, "I planted the seed you gave me and I watered it every day, but it didn't sprout. I put it in a better pot with better soil, but still it didn't sprout. I tended it all year long, but nothing grew. So today I brought an empty pot without a flower. It was the best I could do."

When the Emperor heard those words, a smile spread slowly over his face, and he took Serena by the hand. Serena was frightened. She wondered if she were in some sort of trouble.

The Emperor led her to the front of the Great Hall, and turning to the crowd, he exclaimed: "I have found my successor—the person worthy of ruling after me!"

Serena was puzzled. "But, your Majesty," she said, "I have no flower, just this pot of lifeless earth."

"Yes, I expected that," said the Emperor. "From where everyone else got their seeds, I do not know. The seeds I gave everyone last year had all been roasted. It would have been impossible for any of them to grow. Serena, I admire your great courage and honesty to appear before me with the truth. I reward you with my entire kingdom. You will be the next Empress."

NOTE: *While effort has been made to report the author of this story, we have learned from Librarian Pam Crowell, Harte Library, Long Beach, California, USA, that there are many versions of this ancient tale, and the original author is unknown.*

## Item 7: Happiness
## Story for six- to seven-year-olds

# Billy the Bully

### By John McConnel

Billy was a bully. He was selfish and uncaring and did not think of anyone but himself. He bullied his parents when he wanted an expensive pair of sneakers or a cool new video game. He harassed the other children in school, demanding sweets and money in return for his "protection." He talked back to his teachers and often did not do his lessons. Because people were afraid of him, they disliked him, and that made Billy even more miserable and quarrelsome.

One day when Billy was chasing some boys down the street, he ran smack into Mrs. Johnson and knocked her to the ground. Mrs. Johnson, a frail and elderly woman, was on her way home with a bag of groceries. As she fell to the ground, all of her groceries spilled out. Milk splattered and apples rolled every which way.

At first, Billy charged onward, ignoring the mess he had made. However, when he glanced backward, he noticed something about the way Mrs. Johnson picked herself up off the ground that made him stop and walk back to help her. Mrs. Johnson didn't shout or cry. Instead, she smiled at him and said, "You must be in quite a hurry!" Billy was surprised by her cool attitude and found himself apologizing to her and helping her gather her scattered groceries. Her warmth and gentleness reminded him of his grandmother, who had died when he was a very little boy. He offered to carry her bag, and she gratefully accepted. And so off they went. This was the start of a turning point in Billy's life.

Mrs. Johnson lived in a small house, which was clean and tidy but needed some fixing up. The garden had grown into a jungle. Because Mrs. Johnson had arthritis, she was no longer able to bend down and pull the weeds or mow the lawn. She invited Billy to stay for a cup of cinnamon tea and a piece of homemade cake. "Okay," he said shyly, as he looked around to make sure no one was watching. He was afraid one of his classmates would see him and think that he had gone soft.

Mrs. Johnson introduced him to Skippy, her friendly little dog, and to Tiger, her fat fluffy cat. Before long, Billy was thoroughly enjoying himself, playing with Skippy and Tiger and talking with Mrs. Johnson as if she were his own grandmother. When it was time to leave, Billy was sorry he had to go. This was one of the nicest times he had had in a long time. He tried to think of reasons to stay. Mrs. Johnson also seemed to be thinking as she watched him fumble with his shoestrings. She finally asked, "Would you like to come and visit us again, Billy?"

"Yes, I'd like that," said Billy softly.

As he looked up, Mrs. Johnson's eyes seemed to radiate love and kindness. "You can come by any time, dear," she said.

"Thanks," said Billy, and off he strolled with a smile on his face and a warm glow in his heart. For the first time in longer than he could remember, Billy felt truly happy. For some reason, he felt like singing and being nice to every-one. He even found himself smiling and waving at his arch rival, Wayne, who was passing by on the other side of the road. At first, Wayne seemed a bit startled, but then he smiled back at Billy.

Billy returned to see Mrs. Johnson the next day and the next day after that. Soon his visits became part of his daily routine. He would pop in on his way to school to say "good morning" and to take Skippy for a walk around the block. Mrs. Johnson and Skippy even began to wait for him on the front porch. As Billy approached, Mrs. Johnson would always smile in her warm way and Skippy would bark eagerly. On his way home from school, Billy would stop by to play with Skippy and Tiger and to have a chat with Mrs. Johnson. He would run small errands for her as well. Nothing was too much trouble, as it gave him great joy to help Mrs. Johnson, and she always appreciated his efforts. Over time, he transformed her garden into one of the prettiest in the neighborhood. He was always careful to listen to suggestions and comments.

The more Billy helped Mrs. Johnson, the happier he felt, and the more he wanted to help others. This happy feeling seemed to bubble up inside him and flow outward. He could hardly contain it. He felt so filled with happiness inside that he wanted to "give it away," to share it with others. Billy even started helping out at home, much to his parents' surprise. At school, he stopped his bullying ways and showed himself to be kind, caring and thoughtful. Eventually, he gained everyone's trust, respect and love. He became an example to many. In giving to others, Billy had found a key to happiness.

## Item 8: Tolerance

# Josh the Dragon

### By Diana Hsu

Once upon a time, there lived a big dragon. His name was Josh. One day while Josh was sitting under a big green tree, he thought, "Oh, how nice it would be to have a friend to play with." So that sunny morning, Josh went away, far away, to look for another dragon to be his friend. On his way he met Ethan the elephant.

"Hi," said the elephant with twinkling eyes, "my name is Ethan! What's your name?"

"Josh," he said, "and I'm looking for a friend—a dragon friend, that is." Josh examined Ethan for a moment and then said rather suspiciously, "You have big ears and a long nose. You are not a dragon, are you?"

"No," said the elephant, "but that does not matter, does it? I can still be your friend. You see, I'm looking for a friend, too. I've been feeling sort of lonely lately."

But Josh was not listening to Ethan. He looked at Ethan with coolness and then turned around and trotted off. Ethan, with great sadness, watched Josh leave.

As Josh moved on, he saw a lion. The lion leaped forward with great eagerness, shook his brilliant mane and smiled at Josh. "What are you doing?" he asked.

Josh watched the lion for a moment. Josh had never seen a lion before and was amazed by his beauty. "Oh," he finally replied, "I'm looking for a friend. My name is Josh."

"Oh, I'm looking for a friend, too. My name is Ali, Ali the lion. Come, let's play together. How about having a race or playing a game of tag?" Ali jumped and twirled in anticipation.

At first Josh felt a rush of happiness, but then he suddenly remembered that Ali wasn't a dragon. Josh looked into Ali's smiling face and said, "But you can't be my friend! You are not a dragon." And before the lion could say anything more, Josh turned and ran away.

As Josh was traveling down a country road, he met a little white rabbit. The little rabbit was a bit shy. It hid behind a huge tree, listening carefully with his big long ears and peeking out behind the tree with only one eye. When the little rabbit saw the dragon he thought, "What a big dragon. I hope it's a friendly dragon, otherwise I will have to run away and hide." As Josh came nearer, the little rabbit whispered, "Excuse me, are you a friendly dragon?"

Josh really was a friendly dragon, so the little rabbit did not have to be afraid. He just sat quietly behind the tree and watched Josh. Josh also sat under the same tree where the little rabbit was hiding.

Something very amusing caught Josh's attention just a few trees away. There was a clown laughing with great heartiness as he toppled over his huge shoes. Every time the clown toppled over his feet, he lay on his back and laughed and laughed and laughed. Suddenly, Josh realized that he was laughing too. Like the clown, Josh laughed and laughed and laughed. They both laughed until they had the hiccups, and that made them both laugh even harder. Josh finally got up and went over to the clown and said, "Hi there, you are a funny clown! I never ever in my whole dragon life laughed so much!"

"You are not the only one. Go ask the children, and they will tell you that I make children laugh and laugh and help them forget all their troubles! I love to make people happy. What do you like to do?" asked the jolly clown.

"Well, I'll tell you what I'd like to do," replied Josh in great seriousness. "I'd like to find a friend to play with—a dragon friend, that is."

The clown began to laugh again. "You must be kidding, the whole world can be your friend." The clown laughed and laughed and laughed. Josh suddenly felt embarrassed and a bit sad. He began to feel that no one understood him. He said to himself, "I only want a dragon friend. Is that too much to ask?" So Josh crept back and sat by himself under the tree. As he sat there, two large tears fell from his eyes and rolled down his cheeks. He tried to brush them away, as they began to sting his cheeks.

"Josh, Joshua." He could hear his name being called in the distance. "Are you all right?" As Josh looked up in surprise, he saw Ethan the elephant, Ali the lion, the little white rabbit, and the clown toppling over his shoes and laughing and laughing and laughing. They all surrounded him. Ethan the elephant gently patted his head. Ali the lion licked the salty tears from his red cheeks. The little white rabbit hopped into his lap and nuzzled up against him. And the clown made silly faces until Josh laughed with him. Suddenly, Ali the lion leaped into the air and said gleefully, "Come on, let's play and be happy."

"Yes, let's be happy. You are all my friends!" exclaimed Josh. "You are all my special, special friends. We are all so different and lovely, like the colors of a great big rainbow."

From that moment onward, they were all the best of friends. They shared many wonderful times together. And Josh realized that he would have missed out on all the fun if he had only one dragon friend.

# QUIETLY BEING EXERCISES

## Peace Star Exercise

For a few moments, think of the stars and imagine yourselves to be like them . . . quiet and peaceful. . . . Let the body be still. . . . Relax your toes and legs. . . . Relax your stomach . . . and your shoulders. . . . Relax your arms . . . and your face. . . . You are a Peace Star. . . . What color of peace do you shine with today? . . . perhaps with a rose color that has a feeling of being safe and loved . . . perhaps a blue color that shines a light of peace and courage. . . . We are Peace Stars . . . still . . . full . . . relaxed and peaceful. . . . Whenever you want to feel peaceful inside, you can become very still and quiet inside and remember that you are a Peace Star.

## Respect Star Exercise

For a few moments, be very still. . . . Relax your toes and legs. . . . Relax your stomach . . . and your shoulders. . . . Relax your arms . . . and your face. . . . The Respect Star knows each person brings special qualities to the world. . . . You are a beautiful little star. . . . You are lovable and capable. . . . You are who you are. . . . You are unique and valuable. . . . Enjoy the feeling of respect inside. . . . You are stars of peace that are lovable and capable. . . .

Let yourself be quiet and peaceful inside. . . . Whenever you want to feel especially good inside, be very still inside and remember that you are a star full of peace, a star full of respect.

# Filling Up with Love Exercise

Everyone sit comfortably and let yourself be still inside. . . . Let's pretend there is a soft rose-colored circle of light all around us. . . . That rose light is full of love. . . . That love is so soft and light and safe. . . . That light reminds the light inside of me that it's full of love, too. . . . I tune into that rose light inside me and enjoy the fullness of the love. . . . I am me. . . . I am naturally full of love. . . . I tune into the beauty inside myself. . . . This rose light of love is always there. . . . Whenever I want to feel more love inside, I can tune into that factory of love inside and make lots more.

# CITED BOOKS AND SONGS

## Books

Cohen, Barbara. *Molly's Pilgrim*. New York: Lothrop, Lee and Shepard Books, 1983.

*Living Values: A Guidebook*. San Francisco: Brahma Kumaris, 1995.

Mizumura, Kazue. *Tar and the Tofu*. Cleveland: World Publishing, 1962.

Parkinson, Kathy. *The Enormous Turnip*. Niles, Illinois: A. Whitman, 1986.

Piper, Watty. *The Little Engine That Could*. 60th ed. New York: Platt and Munk, 1990.

Ramsay, Barbara. *Finding the Magic*. Sydney: Eternity Ink, 1995. Available through Global Co-operation House, 65 Pound Lane, London NW10 2HH, UK.

Steptoe, John. *Mufaro's Beautiful Daughters, An African Tale*. New York: Lothrop, Lee and Shepard Books, 1987. This was inspired by a folktale collected by G.M. Theal and published in 1895 in his book, *Kaffir Folktales*.

*The Boy Who Cried Wolf* is sometimes found as a separate illustrated picture book. A facsimile of the 1912 edition is "The Shepherd's Boy and the Wolf." *Aesop's Fables*. New trans. Jones, V.S. Vernon. New York: Avenel Books. Distributed by Crown Publishers.

## Songs

Grammer, Red and Kathy. *Teaching Peace*. New York: Smilin' Atcha Music, 1986. This cassette has a collection of songs created to help children and their parents break down the "big" idea of World Peace into the individual daily actions that will make it a reality. Available from 939 Orchard Street, Peekskill, New York 10566, USA.

*Living Values Songs for Children, Ages 3–7* has the Quietly Being exercises in this book and the following songs: "Each One of Us Is Beautiful," "If Someone Says I Love You," "Happy Children," "The Happy Stars," "My Wings," "Star Songs," "The Rainbow Song" and "Let's Clap Together." Performing Artists: Marneta Viegas, Christine Bell and Alan Beschi. Available through your LVEP Coordinator. (See the LVEP web site at www.livingvalues.net)

Nass, Max and Marcia. *Kindness Songs*. New York: Childswork/Childsplay, 1995. All of the songs on this tape are printed in this book: "Something Kind," "True Blue Friends," "Share," "Smile," "Friends Make the World Go Round" and "In Your Shoes." Available for $7.00 plus shipping. Contact your LVEP Coordinator.

Nass, Max and Marcia. *Songs for Peacemakers*. New York: Activity Records, 1993. This tape includes two songs that were printed in this book with permission from the publishers: "Monster" and "Nice Words." Available from Educational Activities for $11.95, plus shipping. P.O. Box 87, Baldwin, NY 11510 USA. Fax: 1-516-623-9282.

# ACKNOWLEDGMENTS

## To the Educators Who Contributed Values Activities

Dominique Ache and Encarnación Royo Costa developed activities for children ages two through six years in *Manual para Educadores II, Valores para Vivir: Una Iniciativa Educativa, Actividades*. The principal author of the *Manual* was Pilar Quera Colomina. Thank you Pilar, Dominique and Encarnación for your continuing input and support. Thank you, Teresa Garcia Ramos and Carlos Izquierdo Gonzalez, for your stories. Their *Manual* was published by the Spanish Committee of UNICEF and the Brahma Kumaris (1998, ISBN 84 923166 1 6).

Appreciation to Marcia Maria Lins de Medeiros, who contributed values activities that she had done in her work with LVEP in Brazil, and to Tom Bingham for his wonderful role.

Many appreciative regards to John McConnel who heard the request for stories and applied his talents, and to Dana Wilkinson for her editorial support with the stories.

Many thanks to Max and Marcia Nass who lovingly offered their songs and music, and to Marneta Viegas, Christine Bell and Alan Beschi for their cooperation, voices and music in making the Living Values Songs for Children tape.

Frow Steeman of Belgium contributed the beautiful images at the beginning of each values unit. Thank you to David Warrick-Jones for his help with technology.

Thanks to Beverley Crooks, Lygia Monteiro, Helen Sayers and Diana Beaver for their suggestions on the text, to Chris and Amy Farrell for their ideas and support at the beginning of the project, to Pam and Jim Crowel for their help in locating stories, and to Eric Klein for his help with the music on two songs. Appreciation to Diane Holden and Lynn Henshall for their willingness to proofread.

Values activities are a cooperative event!

**And thank you to those reading this
for your interest in and dedication to a better world.**

# ABOUT THE AUTHORS

**Diane G. Tillman** is LVEP's international coordinator for content. A licensed educational psychologist, she is the author of the *Living Values Activities* books for children, young adults, refugees, facilitators and trainers. Diane travels widely internationally, conducting LVEP trainings and lecturing on personal development. Prior to her involvement with LVEP, she worked in a public school system in California for twenty-three years. She has been involved in several international projects for a better world and has served UNA-USA at the local, regional and national levels.

**Diana Hsu** is a teacher who has worked with children aged two through fourteen years for the last twenty-three years in Germany, Hong Kong, Singapore and the United Kingdom. She began writing stories for children ten years ago. The activities and stories she contributed were field tested in several countries for SpARC (Spiritual Application Research Centre). Diana is currently beginning work in London with children who are excluded from school.

# Living Values Series

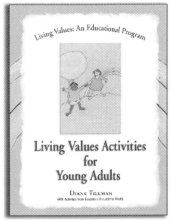

Living Values: An Educational Program

**Living Values Activities for Children Ages 3–7**

DIANE TILLMAN AND DIANA HSU
With Activities from Educators Around the World

Code #8792 • Paperback • $19.95

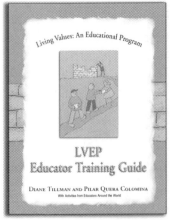

Living Values: An Educational Program

**Living Values Activities for Young Adults**

DIANE TILLMAN
With Activities from Educators Around the World

Code #8814 • Paperback • $19.95

Living Values: An Educational Program

**LVEP Educator Training Guide**

DIANE TILLMAN AND PILAR QUERA COLOMINA
With Activities from Educators Around the World

Code #8830 • Paperback • $12.95

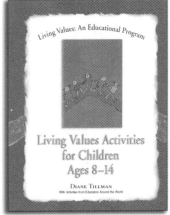

Living Values: An Educational Program

**Living Values Activities for Children Ages 8–14**

DIANE TILLMAN
With Activities from Educators Around the World

Code #8806 • Paperback • $19.95

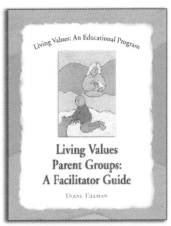

Living Values: An Educational Program

**Living Values Parent Groups: A Facilitator Guide**

DIANE TILLMAN

Code #8822 • Paperback • $10.95

# Growing Souls

### #1 New York Times
BESTSELLING AUTHORS
Jack Canfield
Mark Victor Hansen
with Lisa McCourt

## Chicken Soup for the LITTLE Souls

3 Colorful Stories to
Warm the Hearts
of Children

Code #8121 • Paperback • $12.95

Winner! "Favorite Book"

### #1 New York Times
BESTSELLING AUTHORS
Jack Canfield
Mark Victor Hansen
Patty Hansen
Irene Dunlap

## Chicken Soup for the Kid's Soul

101 Stories of Courage,
Hope and Laughter

Code #6099 • Paperback • $12.95

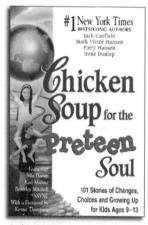

### #1 New York Times
BESTSELLING AUTHORS
Jack Canfield
Mark Victor Hansen
Patty Hansen
Irene Dunlap

## Chicken Soup for the Preteen Soul

101 Stories of Changes,
Choices and Growing Up
for Kids Ages 9–13

Code #8008 • Paperback • $12.95

### #1 New York Times
BESTSELLING AUTHORS
Jack Canfield
Mark Victor Hansen
Kimberly Kirberger

## Chicken Soup for the Teenage Soul II

More
101 Stories of Life, Love
and Learning

Code #6161 • Paperback • $12.95

### #1 New York Times
BESTSELLING AUTHORS
Jack Canfield
Mark Victor Hansen
Kimberly Kirberger

## Chicken Soup for the Teenage Soul

With Outstanding
Stories By
Bill Cosby
Robert Fulghum

101 Stories of
Life, Love and Learning

Code #4630 • Paperback • $12.95

### #1 New York Times
BESTSELLER
Jack Canfield
Mark Victor Hansen
Kimberly Kirberger

## Chicken Soup for the TEENAGE Soul III

More Stories of Life, Love
and Learning

Code #7613 • Paperback • $12.95

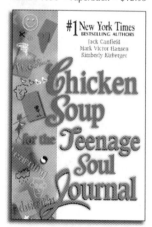

### #1 New York Times
BESTSELLING AUTHORS
Jack Canfield
Mark Victor Hansen
Kimberly Kirberger

## Chicken Soup for the Teenage Soul Journal

Code #6374 • Paperback • $12.95

Available wherever books are sold. To order direct: Phone **800.441.5569** • Online **www.hci-online.com**
Prices do not include shipping and handling. Your response code is **BKS**.

# Books for TEENS

Code #8164 • Paperback • $12.95

Code #6692 • Paperback • $12.95

Code #813X • Paperback • $12.95

Code #9136 • Paperback • $12.95

Code #8334 • Paperback • $11.95

# We Speak Their
# Language

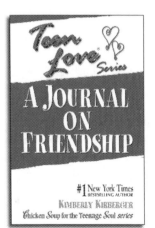

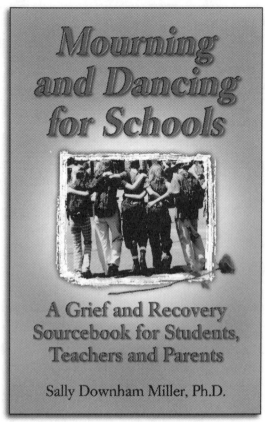

# *Celebrate* Family

*Lessons from Mom* commemorates the timeless wisdom passed from mother to child and is explored in loving detail in this heartwarming collection of stories, essays and poems. With outstanding contributions from Rudyard Kipling, Reba McEntire, Dorothy Parker and many more.

Code #3863 • Paperback • $10.95

*Lessons from Dad* observes the all-important father-child relationship and pays tribute to our greatest teachers, guides and heroes—our dads. With outstanding contributions from Bill Cosby, Gilda Radner, Danny Thomas and many more.

Code #4797 • Paperback • $10.95

*Lessons from Our Children* is a collection of stories, essays and poems that celebrates the bonds of family. With outstanding contributions from Bill Cosby, Kirk Douglas, Christopher Reeve and many more.

Code #6919 • Paperback • $10.95

# Books on Parenting from HCI